# BE STILL
*and*
# BE HAPPY

*devotions for women*

**BroadStreet**
PUBLISHING

BroadStreet Publishing Group, LLC.
Savage, Minnesota, USA
Broadstreetpublishing.com

# BE STILL AND BE HAPPY

978-1-4245-6236-7
978-1-4245-6237-4 (eBook)

Devotional entries composed by Suzanne Niles, Brenna Stockman, and Amy Uecker.

Design by Chris Garborg | garborgdesign.com
Editorial services by Michelle Winger | literallyprecise.com

Printed in China.

21   22   23   24   25   26   28      7   6   5   4   3   2   1

Bless the LORD,
my soul,
And all that
is within me,
bless His holy name!

PSALM 103:1 NASB

# INTRODUCTION

We can choose joy every day when we rely on God to be our source. When we focus on things we are grateful for, our satisfaction in life increases. Comparisons cease. Unnecessary pursuits pause. And we begin to notice the little things. The things that matter. Life. Breath. Kindness. Stillness. Beauty. This is where we find deep connection with God.

As you read these devotions and Scriptures, be inspired to live with gratitude in your heart and praise on your lips. Meditate on things that produce life and peace. Evaluate each day in the light of God's truth and stand in awe of a heavenly Father who gives abundantly more than you can ask or imagine. As you quiet yourself before him, experience the goodness of his presence and be refreshed with his life-giving joy.

# JANUARY

You, dear children, are from God
and have overcome them,
because the one who is in you
is greater than the one
who is in the world.

1 JOHN 4:4 NIV

# PURPOSE

*Many are the plans in a person's heart,*
*but it is the Lord's purpose that prevails.*
PROVERBS 19:21 NIV

It is that famous time of year for making resolutions, examining priorities, and pondering dreams. The Lord's purpose prevails. His goals, priorities, and desires will always stand. Often what we want is different or out of sync with God's plan. At the same time, the relationship between the Lord and us is characterized by love and based on trust. When we desire good things and God seems to withhold them from us, it does not mean he has turned his back on us.

God wants to draw us into a deeper fellowship with him, in and through life's unforeseen circumstances. We can run to the Lord of love with our doubts and fears. We can trust that his plan truly is best. Approach him with open hands and an expectant heart for what he does in your life, both today and in the coming year.

*Lord, I have a lot of plans and desires, and you know the ones that are deep in my heart. I want to trust you with what is ahead. Help me to seek after your heart and your purposes for me.*

# TRUST

*Trust in the LORD with all your heart,*
*And lean not on your own understanding;*
*In all your ways acknowledge Him,*
*And He shall direct your paths.*
PROVERBS 3:5-6 NKJV

The Lord wants our trust in him to be wholehearted. A bungee jumper does not leave the platform with merely halfhearted trust. Our faith in the Lord grows as we get to know him more through his Word. As we see him work through the story of the people of Israel, we realize that his understanding is so much higher and greater than our human minds can contain.

As we seek God's guidance for each decision, he can be counted on to direct us. He uses not only his Word, but also other believers to provide counsel and guidance. His Spirit in us also gives us assurance and peace. What a comfort it is to know that the Lord is with us, holding our hand each step of the journey.

*Lord, thank you for being trustworthy. I ask for your wisdom and guidance. Trying to figure it out on my own is bound to fail me. I place myself in your hands.*

# AUDIENCE OF ONE

*Whatever you do, work heartily,*
*as for the Lord and not for men.*
Colossians 3:23 esv

There is no performance or work required to earn God's love. We could not do a single thing to make God love us any more than he already does (Titus 3:5). His gaze of acceptance is on us as his beloved sons and daughters.

As we increasingly realize the truth of God's delight in us, our heart and attitudes are transformed. We no longer need to watch out of the corner of our eye for a gaze of acceptance from our fellow human beings. What a freedom that brings! May we increasingly desire to please God, pursue excellence in our work, and put our whole heart into everything we do.

*You love me, Lord. What a wonder that is! I want to be so enraptured by your acceptance that I can't help but seek to glorify you. Help me to please you in every task and interaction today.*

# SHINING LIGHT

*"Your light must shine before people in such a way that they may see your good works, and glorify your Father who is in heaven."*
MATTHEW 5:16 NASB

Individuals who need Christ are watching our actions every day, and what we do matters. The purpose of our good deeds is not to score points with God, but instead to point others to the source of our light and life.

Jesus is the light of the world (John 8:12). As he lives in us, we are vessels of his light, hope, and peace. He shows up brightly against the backdrop of the confusion, fear, and hopelessness of this world. We have the privilege of showcasing Christ through the way we live. There is no greater gift we can offer this world than to reflect Jesus and draw others to him.

*Lord, I want your light in me to shine forth. Help me to put you on display through everything I do, simply because you are worthy. Show me where your light is needed in the lives around me.*

# CONNECTION

*If either of them falls down,*
*one can help the other up.*
*But pity anyone who falls*
*and has no one to help them up.*
ECCLESIASTES 4:10 NIV

God created us for relationship. Each of us encounters the Lord in different ways in various seasons. We spur one another on in the body of Christ by sharing in each other's struggles and joys. It might be a victory over a particular sin habit, concern about a personal health issue and how it's challenging our faith, or how a particular passage of Scripture recently spoke to a specific life circumstance.

Sharing on this level involves vulnerability and intentionality. It requires skill and practice in asking good questions and listening well. Prayerfully consider your connections with other believers; maybe someone who could benefit from a deeper communion with you will come to mind.

*Lord, thank you for the blessing of fellow believers you have placed in my life. Show me how to take a step today towards even stronger connection.*

# HE HEARS

*The righteous cry out, and the LORD hears,*
*And delivers them out of all their troubles.*
PSALM 34:17 NKJV

Troubles are an unavoidable part of life in this fallen world. We are not exempt from them simply because we are believers in Jesus. Our deliverer is the living, all-powerful God who is present with us.

In Jesus, we have an advocate who stands before the Father at all times. He hears our heart's cry and wants to come to our aid. He is big enough to handle our honesty when we share how we feel with him. Sometimes his rescue does not look like a miraculous change of circumstances, but instead shows itself as true comfort through his presence. His peace far surpasses our comprehension (Philippians 4:7). Consider the privilege and blessing of having the eager, listening ear of your Savior at any moment.

*Savior, I am so grateful for the privilege of prayer. I can talk to you and cry out to you. Help me to be conscious of your presence with me even in the midst of trouble.*

# ABIDE

*"Abide in me, and I in you. As the branch cannot bear fruit by itself,*
*unless it abides in the vine, neither can you, unless you abide in me."*
JOHN 15:4 ESV

Abiding in Christ means staying connected to him and remaining in him. Just as Jesus, the Son, remained connected to his Father, we should have the same moment-by-moment dependence in fellowship with the Lord. Union with him involves surrendering our will and pursuing his.

As we abide in Jesus, we naturally become fruit bearers. When we think of fruit in Scripture, we often recall the fruit of the Spirit being produced in our hearts: love, joy, peace, patience, kindness, goodness, faithfulness, gentleness, and self-control (Galatians 5:22-23). Bearing fruit also takes on external forms—like the advancing of God's kingdom or bringing lasting change to individual lives. Since our fruitfulness is directly dependent on our connection with Christ, continually cultivate your relationship with him.

*Lord Jesus, I want my life to bear lasting fruit. Show me how to submit more completely to you.*

# OBEDIENCE

*"Devote yourselves completely to the LORD our God, walking in his statutes and keeping his commandments, as at this day."*
1 KINGS 8:61 NRSV

The Lord is worthy of our wholehearted devotion. As our love for him grows, so does our desire to know him through his Word. We cannot hope to obey God's commandments without becoming intimately acquainted with them and meditating on them regularly. As we become familiar with his ways and are changed inwardly by his love, he gives us the desire and grace to obey him in all things. His commands shouldn't be a chore, but rather a delight to follow.

God's commands are perfect and eternal. However, we can never put our hope in the law, or our ability to keep it, to save us. Jesus came to fulfill the law perfectly, to redeem us from slavery under the law, and to make a way for us to be adopted as sons and daughters of God (Galatians 4:3-7).

*Almighty God, thank you for making me your child and redeeming me from enslavement to the law. You are amazing beyond comprehension and perfect in all your ways. Help me to find delight in doing what you want me to do.*

# DELIVERANCE

*"Lead us not into temptation,
but deliver us from the evil one."*
MATTHEW 6:13 NIV

This prayer reveals our dependence upon God to help us remain steadfast in the midst of temptations, trials, and evil. God does not tempt anyone (James 1:13), but he allows us to encounter testing to strengthen our faith. Even Jesus was not exempt. He was tempted in the wilderness by the devil (Matthew 4:1-11). We can always turn to him, knowing that he understands what the experience of temptation feels like.

God is our rescuer, the one we can turn to in any difficulty we face. We cannot resist the power of Satan on our own, but in the Lord, we have the wisdom and power to escape his snares.

*Lord, when you allow testing and trials to come my way, I know you will not abandon me. Give me the faith to hold fast to you.*

# YOUR ACCOUNT

*Each of us will give
an account of himself to God.*
ROMANS 14:12 ESV

When we stand before God on the last day, we will reflect on our lives. We will be answerable to God on an individual basis. A loved one's faith won't be able to save us, and our faith won't be able to cover for anyone else.

God's standard is absolute perfection and holiness. Our own attempts to be right before God utterly fail us, and Scripture compares our attempts at righteousness to dirty rags (Isaiah 64:6). Praise God that, as believers in him, Christ's righteousness has been credited to our accounts. We can draw near to him with confidence.

*Lord of all, you are perfect in holiness. I could never attain your standards, yet through Jesus's sacrifice, you have lifted me to the heights of heaven.*

# GRACE UPON GRACE

*From his fullness we have all received,*
*grace upon grace.*
JOHN 1:16 NRSV

It's impossible to comprehend the abundance of who Christ is and of all we have been given through him. One of those innumerable blessings, grace, is God's favor undeserved, and it grants the power to live a Christian life. Grace does not merely play a role in our salvation; it is for all of life. Whether we have been a believer for a day or for sixty years, we all are dependent on God's grace every day.

Picture a rushing waterfall and what it would feel like to stand directly underneath it. Just as the abundance of water keeps on coming, in Christ we are the recipients of one blessing of grace after another, and we are continuously renewed and strengthened by them.

*Lord, my mind cannot grasp the greatness of who you are. Thank you for the limitless grace you provide to me. Help me to live through your grace and to take joy in your generosity to me.*

# HELD

*Even if my father and mother abandon me,*
*the LORD will hold me close.*
PSALM 27:10 NLT

One of the closest relationships in God's original design is the bond between a parent and child. Sadly, because of the pervasiveness of sin, each of us has experienced hurt of some kind from a parent's failure toward us. Praise God for this great promise from his Word; our heavenly Father will never turn his back on us. In Hebrews 13:5 he says he will never desert or forsake us. In the original language, the wording is emphatic: never, ever, ever will God leave us.

The Lord's posture toward us is described by the beautiful words of "holding me close." May you find comfort in the love and tenderness of God's heart toward you. May brokenness be restored to wholeness in his presence.

*Heavenly Father, not only will you never leave me, but you hold me close in your embrace. I want to stay there, learning how to love like you do.*

# REST

*It is in vain that you rise up early
and go late to rest,
eating the bread of anxious toil;
for he gives to his beloved sleep.*

PSALM 127:2 ESV

Notice the two contrasting themes in this verse: overwork and rest. Forgetting the Lord and striving on our own can take many forms, and one of them may be the life of a workaholic. God designed our minds and bodies to rely on sleep and its renewing effects. Sleep is one of the first things to suffer when we give in to the pressure to be a bigger breadwinner. The Lord wants to replace any fear and anxiety about our material needs with his love, peace, and provision.

If you find yourself anxious about material provision today, may you find assurance through the words of Jesus in Matthew 6:25-34. There, he reminds us that God takes great care of birds and flowers. How much more care will he show to us?

*Lord, show me how to trust you for the provision of my material needs. Help me to be a wise steward of all you have given me, including the blessing of rest.*

# LIVING SACRIFICE

*I plead with you to give your bodies to God because of all he has done for you. Let them be a living and holy sacrifice—the kind he will find acceptable. This is truly the way to worship him.*

ROMANS 12:1 NLT

This word picture is meant to shock us a bit. Human sacrifice is utterly evil, but this verse is about sacrificing our physical bodies by living, not by dying.

In considering God's great compassion toward us, our hearts are drawn to thanksgiving and praise. The highest and truest form of worship that God seeks is that we would willingly offer our lives completely to him. Following Jesus does not mean living our best life now. It costs us something, but it is well worth all we can give (Luke 14:25-33). Consider what it means to surrender your body, mind, soul, and heart to serve God.

*Lord, I am in awe of the mercy you extended to me by sending your Son, Jesus. I want to say thank you by offering my life to you afresh today.*

# ACCEPTANCE

*As it is in your heart, let it be in mine.*
*Christ accepted you, so you should accept each other,*
*which will bring glory to God.*

ROMANS 15:7 NCV

The theme of this passage is unity among believers. We are to accept one another because we are the recipients of unconditional acceptance from Christ. Acceptance of one another does not mean undiscerning agreement. It means accepting someone as a person, laying aside any personal prejudice.

We are to bear with each other's character traits and life background as well as personal convictions on "gray areas": for example, personal standards on drinking alcohol, how much, and when it's okay. Getting to know one another deeply will aid us in our quest to not unintentionally lead someone down a path toward sin.

*Lord, give me discernment in my interactions with others in the body of Christ. Help my relationships to bring you glory and provide instruction to others.*

# WINNING

*Do you not know that in a race all the runners run,*
*but only one gets the prize?*
*Run in such a way as to get the prize.*
1 Corinthians 9:24 NIV

We are exhorted by Paul the apostle to pursue excellence in our life with Christ, just as a professional athlete strives to win. The race requires endurance, discipline, and training (1 Corinthians 9:27). It takes a commitment to never call it quits.

Praise God that we are not in competition with each other for God's affection. We could never earn his favor through our own striving. Our adoption into God's family—the ultimate prize—has already been won for us through Jesus. We strive to please God out of thanksgiving for all he has done for us. Our whole life ought to reflect the goodness and mercy of God, shown through our continual growth and pursuit to bring him glory.

*Lord, show me where I need more training and greater endurance in my spiritual life. Thank you that the best prize of all is already mine through your Son.*

# FORGIVENESS

*"Whenever you stand praying,*
*forgive, if you have anything against anyone;*
*so that your Father in heaven*
*may also forgive you your trespasses."*
MARK 11:25 NRSV

We are no different from anyone else in that we are sinners in need of forgiveness. In our redemption, God has shown us mercy we did not earn or deserve (Ephesians 2:4-5).

It would be like setting ourselves higher than God if we withheld mercy from those who have done wrong to us. See Matthew 18:21-35 for a poignant illustration that Jesus gave about forgiveness. The ability to forgive can be extremely difficult on our own, but we can ask the Lord, our example and grace-giver, for his power to do the impossible.

*Lord, I need your help to forgive from the heart when others offend me. I don't want any grudge I may be holding to get in the way of my prayer life.*

# WHEN LIFE HURTS

*Give thanks in all circumstances;
for this is the will of God in Christ Jesus for you.*
1 THESSALONIANS 5:18 ESV

Giving thanks in all situations is easier said than done. We would rather just give thanks when we are happy and content. Uncomfortable, pain-filled circumstances tend to evoke little thanks and praise to God, unless he gives us the grace to seek out what he's doing under the surface.

A surgeon's scalpel brings pain for a time, but its purpose is to bring about improved health. In the same way that we can trust a surgeon's skill, we can trust our all-knowing, all-powerful God in the midst of heartache. God knows what we are facing. We can trust that he is allowing it for his purposes, even if we don't understand why. These are precisely the times that can highlight our dependence on God and cause us to grow in our faith the most.

*Lord, help me to thank and praise you even when life hurts. You are always worthy, even when I don't understand your plan.*

# CREATION

*God created great sea creatures and every living thing that scurries and swarms in the water, and every sort of bird—each producing offspring of the same kind. And God saw that it was good.*
GENESIS 1:21 NLT

Through creation, God demonstrated his sovereign power over the world and everything in it. He created each of the numerous species of fish and birds on the fifth day of creation. God designed each of them, with their wide variety of colors, shapes, and habits. It's easy to imagine that God instilled creation with beauty and diversity purely for his own, and our, pleasure.

"God saw that it was good" implies that God took delight in his own handiwork. Before sin and its consequences entered the world, it truly was good and perfect. We as God's image bearers also have great capacity for creativity. We can use the gift of creativity to glorify God and point others toward our Maker.

*God, I praise you for the beauty of your creation that I get to enjoy. Help me to use my creativity in ways that honor you and bless others.*

# LOVE AND OBEDIENCE

*"If you love me,
obey my commandments."*
JOHN 14:15 NLT

Before discussing obedience, there is an important sequence to understand. This verse is preceded by Jesus' urging listeners to believe in him (John 14:10-11). We believe first, and then Jesus entreats us to love him. The basis of our love and devotion to the Lord is that he first loved us.

Picture starry-eyed newlyweds. Out of sheer love, the husband lives for and delights to make his new wife happy. He's willing to do whatever he can to fulfill her requests, and the same goes for his wife. They are continuously discovering each other's likes and dislikes so that they can do little acts of service for each other. Likewise, out of love and thanksgiving for all Jesus is to us, we will want to know his will and seek it.

*Lord, your unfailing love for me exceeds that of the most passionate lover. I want to love and obey you from my heart.*

# WAITING

*Those who wait for the LORD shall renew their strength,*
*they shall mount up with wings like eagles,*
*they shall run and not be weary,*
*they shall walk and not faint.*
ISAIAH 40:31 NRSV

Waiting on God indicates trusting him to act. It means not taking matters into our own hands.

We may be waiting for clarity and direction or for answers to prayer. Often, God's timetable appears slower than ours. If we aren't watchful, we may rush ahead of God.

Striving on our own leads to mental and emotional exhaustion. In choosing trust, we find renewed strength and courage. Lean into the beauty of these word pictures. Let your mind's eye find the eagle soaring effortlessly on the breeze, the runner's legs pumping without tiring or losing breath. It's a restful, freeing place to live.

*Lord, striving without you wears me out. Help me to find rest as I choose to trust and wait on your timing.*

# OUR FOREVER HOME

*Since we believe that Jesus died and rose again, even so, through Jesus, God will bring with him those who have fallen asleep.*

1 THESSALONIANS 4:14 ESV

We worship the living, risen Christ. We must not stop at the crucifixion, but instead continue to the third day when Jesus was raised from the dead and appeared bodily to many (Luke 24). He ascended to heavenly glory and is now seated at the right hand of the Father.

We have a glorious hope through the resurrection of Jesus. Because he defeated death, we as believers in him will likewise not stay in the grave. For us, death has lost its sting. Believers in Jesus who have preceded us in death are in now God's presence (2 Corinthians 5:8). One day, when our appointed time comes, we will join them. Heaven is our forever home. Whenever you are reminded of the brevity and tenuous nature of this earthly life, may you be comforted by this promise.

*Lord, thank you for the resurrection and for the promise that I have an eternal home with you in heaven.*

# SACRIFICIAL LOVE

*"I am giving you a new commandment,*
*that you love one another;*
*just as I have loved you,*
*that you also love one another."*

JOHN 13:34 NASB

This passage in John's gospel is spoken just hours before Jesus goes to the cross. Physically following Jesus used to be the mark of being his disciple. Since Jesus will soon be absent from them, the new indication will be the love they have for one another. When others witness that kind of love, they will know these men are his disciples (John 13:35).

Jesus is commanding us to love each other with the same kind of love that he has for us. Going to the cross on our behalf was the ultimate act of selfless love. It may seem unreasonable for Jesus to ask us to love our fellow believers in this way, and it would not be possible apart from the power of God. The same power that raised Jesus from the dead is now at work in us who believe (Romans 8:11). Being a follower of Jesus leads to inner heart transformation, which will manifest in our outward behavior towards one another in the family of God.

*Lord, I'm amazed by your sacrificial love for me. Help me to lay down my own agenda to love and serve my brothers and sisters in Christ.*

# UNBURDENING

*Cast your burden on the Lord,*
*And He shall sustain you;*
*He shall never permit the righteous to be moved.*
PSALM 55:22 NKJV

God knows everything about our lives and our unique concerns. He is not far off and aloof. He wants us to pour out our hearts to him and unburden ourselves in his presence. When troubles pop up, often we would turn first to a friend or loved one to vent our frustration and disappointment. How much better it would be to first run to the Lord, who cares more than any human being could.

In letting God take our burdens, we find the promise of the Lord's sustaining power. His grace will always be sufficient for every situation. To never permit us to be shaken doesn't mean that he won't let anything bad happen to us. It means he won't allow our faith to be destroyed. We can't rely on our subjective feelings to determine our standing with God. When we feel we are sinking in quicksand, his Word is our sure foundation.

*Lord, I want to bring the burdens of my heart to you. Help me to trust you and sustain me by your grace when everything feels shaky.*

# MERCY

*"They are blessed who show mercy to others,*
*for God will show mercy to them."*
MATTHEW 5:7 NCV

This is near the opening of Jesus' famous sermon on the mount. Through the Beatitudes, he appeals to our desire for happiness and blessing. The route to obtaining that happiness is so different from the world's message to pursue wealth, power, and fame. Jesus' desire for us is to completely transform our hearts.

Extending mercy and acting in kindness to others when they don't deserve it goes against human nature. When we have a keen awareness of our own sinfulness and of our dependence upon God's mercy, it enables us to go against the tide. If we have experienced God's mercy and compassion, we can show mercy to others. We have the privilege of being the extension of Christ's mercy and compassion to this world that desperately needs him.

*Lord, you have shown me great mercy and compassion. Help me to be merciful to those who don't deserve it. None of us deserve mercy, and yet you offer it freely.*

# COMMUNICATION

*Take note of this: Everyone should be quick to listen,*
*slow to speak and slow to become angry.*
JAMES 1:19 NIV

Many of us would much rather talk than listen to what others have to say. This verse is for all of us, not just the loudmouths. Being a good listener requires a degree of humility. In order to truly listen well, we must consciously put a pause on our own thoughts and consider the speaker before ourselves.

Being slow to speak does not mean being reticent and shy. This verse is referring to contemplating a thought, especially a word of advice or admonition, before sharing it. As we mature in our faith, we ought to become less self-righteous and more aware of our own weaknesses. We also should become less defensive and indignant when others confront us or disagree with our point of view.

*Lord, help me to be a loving listener and to grow in humility, wisdom, and gentleness in my communication with others.*

# PERMANENCE

*When God chooses someone and graciously imparts gifts to him,*
*they are never rescinded.*

ROMANS 11:29 TPT

The gifts that this verse refers to are not the blessings that he sometimes gives us for a time, such as health or prosperity. Those kinds of gifts are not guaranteed, nor are they permanent. Here, it's referring to spiritual realities: the blessings of salvation, grace, adoption, eternal life, and so many more.

The call to salvation and all of the spiritual blessings God gives are permanent. God never changes his mind or goes back on his word. God himself does not change; he is "the same yesterday, today, and forever" (Hebrews 13:8). We can rest in the knowledge that our spiritual inheritance is forever.

*Lord, when I am tempted to doubt my salvation or my spiritual standing, help me to remember that I am yours forever, because of who you are.*

# COURAGE

*Be strong, and let your heart take courage,*
*all you who wait for the LORD!*
PSALM 31:24 ESV

At the close of this psalm, David the psalmist encourages us based on his own experience of God's faithfulness. He urges us to not give up our hope in God in the face of trying times. When we feel ready to give in and yield to fear and doubt, we need the voice of encouragement to spur us on. The book of Psalms is a great place to run to when we need to keep our courage up.

When we feel weak, we can be strong in the strength the Lord provides. In fact, it is in the times we come to the end of ourselves that God is best able to meet us in our need (2 Corinthians 12:9-10). Don't give up hope! The Lord is always faithful.

*Lord, I need you! I feel weak, but you are strong. Help me to not stop putting my hope in you.*

# WIND AND WAVES

*They were filled with great fear and said to one another,*
*"Who then is this, that even the wind and the sea obey him?"*
MARK 4:41 ESV

In the midst of the storm, it's easy to get caught up in the problems that face us. Our default mode wants to focus on the height of the waves and lose sight of all else, especially Jesus. His timing and manner of resolution may be entirely different from our desires, but we can rest in the assurance that all is under his authority.

The disciples appear so fickle in this passage in Mark. Their fear of drowning in the storm quickly turns to fear, awe, and respect for Jesus, but only after he rebukes the storm, and all is calm. Recognize a similar tendency to doubt in your own heart. Then, return to a place of trust and awe, and rest in Christ's care for you.

*Jesus, just as you spoke to the wind and waves from the boat, I know you are with me. I can trust you with any problems I face today.*

# SALVATION

*If you confess with your mouth the Lord Jesus and believe in your heart that God has raised Him from the dead, you will be saved. For with the heart one believes unto righteousness, and with the mouth confession is made unto salvation.*

ROMANS 10: 9-10 NKJV

Salvation here indicates rescue from the penalty for sin, which is separation from God forever. Our salvation is found by grace through faith, not by works (Ephesians 2:8-9). The very meaning of the name Jesus is salvation, and it is because of his death and resurrection that the door to God's rescue is flung wide open.

We can see that there is both an inward aspect to faith as well as an outward confession. First, the inward reality is belief and trust from the heart. Secondly, the outward confession to others confirms where we stand. This confession reveals itself in how we act and the choices we make. Our lives experience change on such a fundamental level, and it affects everything we do, including the words we speak.

*Jesus, thank you for being my rescue. I believe in you as my only Savior and Lord. May my life and my words reflect how you have worked within my heart.*

# PEACEMAKING CITIZENS

*Remind the people to be subject to rulers and authorities, to be obedient, to be ready to do whatever is good, to slander no one, to be peaceable and considerate, and always to be gentle toward everyone.*

TITUS 3:1-2 NIV

Our adherence to God in our spiritual lives does not negate the need for obedience to earthly rulers. Romans 13:1 reminds us that our rulers in government have been put in place by God. We are to be exemplary citizens and obedient to the governing officials and laws, as long as those mandates are not in violation of God's Word.

We are to not speak evil of anyone, even if we ourselves experience mistreatment and slander from others for following Christ. As believers, we ought to be makers of peace, not discord. By our humility and gentleness, we can bring calm to the hotheaded conflict that typically characterizes this world. By acting differently, we are a living testimony to the power of God.

*Lord, I need your grace. Help me to obey the authorities and to be a peacemaker in this land. Give me a humble heart will yield to you.*

# FEBRUARY

You, O Lord, are a shield about me,

my glory, and the lifter of my head.

PSALM 3:3 ESV

# WITHOUT SIN

*When they persisted in asking Him,*
*He straightened up, and said to them,*
*"He who is without sin among you,*
*let him be the first to throw a stone at her."*

JOHN 8:7 NASB

The Pharisees caught a woman in the act of adultery. They brought her before Jesus to see if he would condemn her and call for her stoning. They were using her to try to trap Jesus in wrongdoing and then make formal accusations against him before the authorities.

Instead of giving a direct reply, Jesus shows his superior wisdom by declaring that whoever is without sin should throw the first stone. One at a time the accusers all leave, realizing they are just as guilty. Jesus alone could claim to be without sin, and yet he does not throw a single stone. Jesus demonstrates his mercy and care for this woman and urges her to leave her life of sin. His heart of mercy is the same toward us.

*Lord, thank you for your mercy on me in my own sin struggles. Give me the strength to lay aside sinful habits and find fulfillment in you.*

# TRUE RICHES

*My God will supply every need of yours*
*according to his riches in glory in Christ Jesus.*
PHILIPPIANS 4:19 ESV

The Philippian church gave generously to support the apostle Paul's material needs as a minister of the gospel. Here, Paul is writing to thank the church and to encourage them. This verse is no firm guarantee that those who follow God will prosper materially. In fact, just a few verses before, Paul talks about how he has had times of going hungry.

Paul is saying that God will supply everything we need to be content in the Lord. His confidence is in the unfailing grace of God. Out of the spiritual abundance of Christ, and because of a faith firmly rooted in him, he will give us the grace to find our ultimate satisfaction in him, no matter what our circumstances are.

*You are my treasure, Lord. Thank you for the promise that your supply of grace will never run dry. Help me to learn the secret of contentment in you.*

# CHILDLIKE FAITH

*The LORD protects those of childlike faith;*
*I was facing death, and he saved me.*
PSALM 116:6 NLT

Being childlike is different from being childish. Young children are generally teachable, unassuming, and trusting. God's favor rests on those who humble themselves like a child (Matthew 18:3-4). He wants us to depend on him completely, just as children possess a carefree dependence on their parents.

When we come to the end of ourselves and acknowledge our weakness, we are then able to receive the help that the Lord longs to give us. He takes delight in caring for us, his beloved children. Isaiah 42:3 says he will not break a bruised reed. None of us are so broken as to be beyond hope. He will not leave us defenseless; he will come to our aid.

*Lord, over and over again you have shown yourself faithful in times of trouble. Help me to remember that when I feel weak, I can depend on you to give me strength.*

# LONGING FOR GOD

*One thing I ask from the LORD, this only do I seek:*
*that I may dwell in the house of the LORD all the days of my life,*
*to gaze on the beauty of the LORD and to seek him in his temple.*

PSALM 27:4 NIV

When David wrote this psalm many years before Christ's coming, the temple or tabernacle was the place where God's presence dwelled. David isn't speaking about wanting to physically take up residence in the temple. He is conveying his adoration for the Lord and his desire to continually remain conscious of God's presence.

David went beyond asking for anything God can provide; he expressed his heart's longing simply for God himself. Psalm 16:11 says that God's presence is where we experience abundantly satisfying joy. We as God's children always have a home with our heavenly Father, and we long for the day when we will see him face to face. Contemplate the beauty of the Lord and all of his wonderful attributes. Pour out your love and worship to him and be filled with joy in his presence.

*Good Father, you are beautiful and perfect in all your ways. I take delight in knowing you and being near you.*

# MIRACLE WORKER

*You are the God who performs miracles;*
*you display your power among the peoples.*
PSALM 77:14 NIV

Our God is like no other. He is the God who works wonders of all kinds (Exodus 15:11). He delivered the Israelites from slavery in Egypt. He parted the Red Sea and provided food and water in the desert. His supernatural care and provision were so far above any other god that the Lord's fame spread to all the surrounding nations.

God's miraculous power is constantly at work all around us. His supernatural power is seen in nature, miracles of healing, and divine protection from physical harm. His wonder-working strength is displayed in the changed hearts and lives of sinners. He has liberated us from bondage to sin and its consequences. God desires to spread his fame to all nations and people groups, that they might come to know and believe in him.

*Lord, you are the God who works wonders. Thank you for redeeming my life and making me a new person. Show me how I can help spread your fame to the nations that do not yet know your name.*

# HEART MOTIVES

*"Be careful! When you do good things,
don't do them in front of people to be seen by them.
If you do that, you will have no reward from your Father in heaven."*

MATTHEW 6:1 NCV

The good works we do are the evidence that our faith is alive, according to James 2:14-26. Therefore, good deeds are a vital aspect of our lives as believers. The average person living in biblical times would have considered the Pharisees to be exemplary in their righteous living. However, the Pharisees were also known for making a show of their good deeds.

Today's admonition from Jesus reaches the level of our hearts, testing our motivations for why we perform acts of kindness. If we believe that our righteousness rests on Christ, we won't need to seek the approval of other people. In Philippians 2:12-13, we see that it is God working in us that grants the impetus and the strength to do anything good. In view of God's grace toward us, our deeds become a spontaneous outpouring of praise to the Lord.

*Lord, you have already accepted me by your grace and the gift of your righteousness. I want my deeds to be acts of praise to you.*

# TRUE CONFIDENCE

*Do not throw away your confidence,*
*which has a great reward.*
HEBREWS 10:35 NCV

This passage is about persevering in the midst of difficulty and suffering. The word "confidence" here is referring to confident trust and hope in the Lord. If our confidence is merely in ourselves, we will falter. The world has plenty of examples of self-confidence. However, our confidence as believers must rest on the Lord and his faithfulness.

To throw away one's confidence could be compared to a soldier tossing his weapons aside and running away from the battle. Although we may be inwardly quaking because of the spiritual battles and trials we face, let us not give up hope in the Lord. Perseverance grows as our faith is put to the test. As a result, we grow stronger in our faith and in our inner character. Stay the course and don't give up, and your perseverance will lead to great reward.

*Lord, sometimes I feel like giving up when I can't see an end to the trials I'm facing. Even if I falter, help me to not give up hoping in you.*

# DILIGENT STUDY

*Do your best to present yourself to God as one approved,*
*a worker who has no need to be ashamed,*
*rightly handling the word of truth.*
2 Timothy 2:15 esv

Paul wrote to encourage Timothy to be diligent in his role as a Christian worker. Likewise, we are to serve the Lord with the goal of pleasing him rather than to gain the favor of people. This exhortation applies to every believer, not just pastors and Bible teachers in a formal setting. We all should seek opportunities to grow alongside of others in the family of faith and to share what we are learning from the Bible.

We should carefully handle God's Word, first to apply it to our own lives, and then to benefit other believers that we influence. Take care to examine and stay true to the intended meaning of Scripture, and don't infuse it with your preconceived ideas. The discovery process involves studying to understand the wider context of a particular verse. If you are new to studying the Bible, seek out a wise helper.

*Lord, help me to be an eager student of your Word and apply it correctly. Let it bear fruit in my life and in those around me.*

# RADICAL LOVE

*"Love your enemies, and do good,*
*and lend, expecting nothing in return,*
*and your reward will be great,*
*and you will be sons of the Most High,*
*for he is kind to the ungrateful and the evil."*
LUKE 6:35 ESV

It's easy to like those who like us in return. We are naturally drawn to perform acts of kindness for those in our circle of acquaintance. In his teaching, Jesus pointed out that even those living in sin are capable of loving others when there is an expectation of personal benefit.

However, Jesus is asking us to act contrary to our human nature. He is calling us to love those who don't like us. He wants us to be imitators of the Most High God, who loves and accepts us unconditionally. His mercy is for us, with no strings attached. God wants to highlight his goodness through us, his children, so that the world can see what he is like.

*Lord, thank you for loving me even though I don't deserve it. Give me grace to love those I deem unlovable, without expecting anything in return.*

# A HIGHER AUTHORITY

*Peter and the apostles replied,*
*"We must obey God rather than any human."*
ACTS 5:29 NLT

The chief priests in Jerusalem arrested the apostles. They commanded them to stop teaching the people that Jesus is the Son of God. The Lord miraculously set them free from prison, and they immediately resumed teaching about Jesus. They had no thought of stopping. When the chief priests brought them in for questioning a second time, they were baffled at the apostles' choice to disobey their command.

The apostles were firm in the knowledge that they were doing exactly what God wanted them to do. We are to respect those in government and obey them. At the same time, God's law is higher than any other, so his will is the supreme guide for our conduct. Love compels us to share the hope we have in Jesus, no matter what the law of the land says. May we have the apostles' resolve to boldly share Christ.

*Lord, give me the courage and the heart to share about you, no matter what anyone else says.*

# NEW CREATION

*If anyone is in Christ, there is a new creation:*
*everything old has passed away;*
*see, everything has become new!*

2 CORINTHIANS 5:17 NRSV

To be "in Christ" is to be united with him. Those of us who have come to faith in Jesus are new creations. Our motivations, desires, and longings are changed to such a degree that it is as if we become completely different people. We no longer have the same appetites, and now we find satisfaction in belonging to God.

Today's verse is both a declaration of truth and a promise. Whatever characterized our life before meeting Jesus is now forgotten. Psalm 103:12 says God removes our sins from us as far as the east is from the west. In Jeremiah 31:34, we read that God's forgiveness is so complete, it is as if God blots out the memory of our sin. He is the God of second chances and redemption. Reflect upon this truth in light of your own life and that of others around you.

*Lord, thank you for making me a new person through your grace. I will never be the same again!*

# CONTENTMENT

*I know what it is to be in need, and I know what it is to have plenty.*
*I have learned the secret of being content in any and every situation,*
*whether well fed or hungry, whether living in plenty or in want.*
PHILIPPIANS 4:12 NIV

Contentment seems foreign to the world's idea of keeping up with the status quo. Our culture continually feeds us the line, "If you just had more, then you would be happy." However, we who have put our faith in Christ have realized the hollowness of that message.

In Matthew 6:33, Jesus tells us that seeking God's kingdom is our ultimate quest. In his kingdom, we find that Jesus satisfies the deepest longings of our hearts. Encountering him ends our search for love, acceptance, and fulfillment. We will not be anxious when we encounter seasons of need if we truly trust the Lord for provision. The next verse in Paul's letter to the Philippians is: "I can do all this through him who gives me strength." It reminds us that the Lord gives us the strength to remain content in him in every season.

*Lord, you alone satisfy the deepest longings of my heart.*
*I look to you for provision, whether in times of need or*
*abundance.*

# LISTENING TO GOD

*Search me, O God, and know my heart;*
*test me and know my anxious thoughts.*
PSALM 139:23 NLT

This psalm of David begins by his description of how thoroughly God knows our thoughts, words, and actions. At first glance, we may wonder why David would then write this prayer asking God to know his thoughts.

David was asking God to reveal to him the state of his own heart. Sometimes, we do not fully comprehend our own motives or understand the source of our fears. We do not know ourselves as well as the Lord, our Creator, knows us. We can count on the Lord to show us where we have stumbled into sin and guide us to repentance. We have the help of the Word and the Holy Spirit to teach and guide us (2 Timothy 3:16). Being open to the Lord's prompting takes time and space to listen. Jesus himself took time away to be with God in prayer (Luke 5:16). Prayer should be a two-way conversation.

*Lord, I need your help to understand the state of my own heart. Help me to be sensitive to the prompting of your Spirit.*

# GOD IS LOVE

*Beloved, let us love one another, for love is of God;
and everyone who loves is born of God and knows God.
He who does not love does not know God, for God is love.*

1 JOHN 4:8 NKJV

"God is love" highlights how thoroughly love characterizes God's nature. He loves, but he goes a step further. He is the very essence and definition of love. Those who want to know what love is will find the answer to their quest in the person of Jesus.

This same love characterizes those who have new life in Christ: those who are "born of God" and have become his. When we are connected to God and transformed by his love, he works in such a way that love defines who we are as well. Someone who has meager love for others is little acquainted with God. Therefore, let love reign in your relationships with your brothers and sisters in Christ and with all you meet.

*Lord, help me to be increasingly transformed by your love and characterized by your love flowing through me.*

# HEART TRANSPLANT

*"I will give them one heart, and put a new spirit within them.*
*And I will remove the heart of stone from their flesh*
*and give them a heart of flesh."*

EZEKIEL 11:19 NASB

God has an active role in creating spiritual renewal in the people of Israel and in our lives today. The symbolism about God performing heart surgery on us shows that we can't do this ourselves. At the same time, it is clear from Ezekiel 18:31 that we are commanded to make ourselves a new heart by putting our faith in the Lord. Both God's role and our response are at work.

A heart of stone is unreceptive, dead, and unfeeling toward God. Apart from God, we are hopeless. We don't need quadruple bypass surgery; we need a total heart transplant. The kindness of God leads us to repentance (Romans 2:4). We who are in Christ are now soft-hearted and receptive to the Lord, and we become conduits of his life. As you think about those you know who need Christ, be mindful of the miraculous heart transplant required.

*Lord, what a miracle you have worked in my heart! I look to you to soften the hardest hearts in those around me.*

# AGAINST THE FLOW

*Those who live only to satisfy their own sinful nature will harvest decay and death from that sinful nature. But those who live to please the Spirit will harvest everlasting life from the Spirit. So let's not get tired of doing what is good. At just the right time we will reap a harvest of blessing if we don't give up.*

GALATIANS 6:8-9 NLT

Living to please our sinful desires seems as natural as breathing. It's our default mode without the grace of God. "If it feels good, do it," is the world's decree for behavior in regard to relationships, finances, sexuality, and countless other areas of daily life.

However, we are in Christ and therefore we live to please the Spirit, rather than ourselves. It's hard to go against the current, and it often seems impossible. It takes a continual dependence upon God's grace, asking him to give us wisdom in the daily decisions we face. Let's not get tired, but instead continue to persevere in the same way we began our new life with Christ, keeping our focus on him (Hebrews 12:1-3). Press onward and upward!

*Lord, give me your grace to live in a way that pleases you. When the going gets tough, help me to persevere in your strength.*

# SPIRITUAL BATTLE

*Submit therefore to God.*
*But resist the devil,*
*and he will flee from you.*
JAMES 4:7 NASB

The devil is real. He is a fallen angel who rebelled against God (see Ezekiel 28 and Isaiah 14) and is now his enemy. He seeks to deceive God's followers and destroy all that he upholds. A clear example of his cunning deceptions is found at the very beginning, in Genesis.

Satan likes to appeal to our pride and submitting ourselves to God's will is the antidote. In submitting ourselves to God, we acknowledge his lordship and our humble dependence on him. We can claim the promise of Romans 8:38 that no evil power can separate us from the love of God. As God's children, we have the victory over Satan's schemes because God is stronger than Satan. We are in a battle in the unseen, spiritual realm, but we have the resources of the Lord at our disposal. Put on your armor for the battle and claim the victory that is already yours through Jesus.

*Lord, I submit to you anew today. Thank you for winning the victory over Satan all those years ago. No one can separate me from your love.*

# ANGER AND RECONCILIATION

*"In your anger do not sin":*
*Do not let the sun go down while you are still angry,*
*and do not give the devil a foothold.*
EPHESIANS 4:26-27 NIV

Anger is like the engine warning light on a car. It can signal that something deeper is going on in our hearts. Often what lurks behind anger is selfish motivations. If we allow anger to become our habit, trouble and wrongdoing are sure to come along for the ride. James 1:20 says that our anger does not produce righteousness.

God is very specific about relinquishing our anger quickly, ideally within 24 hours. Part of the reason is to avoid giving Satan traction in our hearts. Nursing a grudge against an offending person may temporarily feel good, but God wants us to confess and forgive one another in a timely way. Surrender your own desires, and if it is within your power, make the first step toward resolution. Ultimately, you are bringing glory to God, and he delights in the sweetness of reconciliation.

*Lord, help me to have a heart for reconciliation when conflicts arise, and to lay down any grudges against others who offend me.*

# RUNNING THE RACE

*Since we are surrounded by so great a cloud of witnesses,*
*let us also lay aside every weight and the sin that clings so closely,*
*and let us run with perseverance the race that is set before us.*
HEBREWS 12:1 NRSV

The previous chapter, Hebrews 11, recounts the faith of many people throughout the pages of Scripture, including Noah, Abraham, Moses, and many others. Through this overview, we can almost picture the heroes of the faith in the stands, watching and cheering us on. Knowing they persevered by faith gives us encouragement to keep on running the race.

A professional runner carefully suits up before a race; every piece is designed for the necessary speed. Continuing in old sin habits would be like a runner trying to enter the race while wearing a flowing robe. Sin weighs us down and hinders our progress in the Christian life. Consider whether a particular habitual sin may be tripping you up. Confess, repent, and turn to Jesus. Look full in his face and gain renewed endurance for the race called life.

*Lord, I'm encouraged by the stories of those who have gone before me in the life of faith. Help me to lay aside sinful habits, and I ask for renewed strength and endurance.*

# PURSUED BY LOVE

*Surely your goodness and unfailing love
will pursue me all the days of my life,
and I will live in the house of the Lord forever.*

PSALM 23:6 NLT

The Lord is our Good Shepherd, and we are his sheep, the flock he faithfully and tenderly guards and keeps in his care. As members of the flock of God, we can be confident of his wise provision and goodness. No matter what trouble comes our way or how dark the valley may be that God leads us through, we don't have to fear because God is with us (Psalm 23:4). His loving presence is our greatest treasure.

As members of this special flock, it is not a dangerous predator that is continually hounding us. Instead, it is God himself who constantly pursues us with his love, kindness, and compassion. His relationship with us is forever. We have the privilege of enjoying him now and for eternity.

*Lord, you are my Good Shepherd. I'm amazed by your unfailing and generous love for me.*

# JUSTIFIED

*Since we have been justified by faith,*
*we have peace with God through our Lord Jesus Christ.*
ROMANS 5:1 ESV

Our Lord is a God of perfect justice. He does not show favoritism to one particular group over another (Deuteronomy 32:4). God is perfectly holy and cannot allow evil in his presence. Since we are sinners, we deserve death and separation from God (Romans 6:23).

Being justified means we are put in right standing with God. Because of our faith in Jesus and because of his death and resurrection, we are acquitted of our guilt. We are liberated from the punishment we deserve for our sin. We no longer stand condemned before God, our holy and just judge. Instead of receiving his wrath, we have peace with God. By sending his own Son to the cross, God the Father drew us to him. Now we belong to him, and we can come boldly and unashamedly to the very throne of God.

*Dear Father, you sent your Son to pay the price for my sin. Through Jesus, you opened the way for me to be restored to you. Thank you for this priceless gift.*

# FEAR TO TRUST

*In God, whose word I praise,*
*In God I have put my trust;*
*I shall not be afraid.*
*What can mere mortals do to me?*

PSALM 56:4 NASB

David wrote Psalm 56 when the Philistines—the enemy—had seized him. He had every reason to be afraid for his life. In fact, David acknowledged his fear in verse three when he wrote, "When I am afraid, I will put my trust in you." The foundation of David's, and therefore our, trust in God is found in his Word. We can put our confidence in what God says.

It's easy to lose sight of the bigger picture of eternity when we are in the midst of danger, including threats from our fellow human beings. However, Matthew 10:28 reminds us that mere mortals don't have the power to destroy our souls, which are of primary importance in light of eternity. God is for us, so we have nothing to fear from those who would stand against us. We can hold onto the promises of God in the midst of terror-inducing events.

*Lord, thank you for your promises that I can hang onto in the midst of my fear. Help me to put my trust in you.*

# JESUS IS ARRESTED

*"Put your sword back in its place," Jesus said to him,*
*"for all who draw the sword will die by the sword.*
*Do you think I cannot call on my Father,*
*and he will at once put at my disposal*
*more than twelve legions of angels."*

MATTHEW 26:52-53 NIV

This passage comes from the hours before Jesus was crucified, when the temple guards came to arrest him. Peter, attempting to stand up in Jesus' defense, had just drawn his sword and cut off the high priest's servant's ear (John 18:10), and his Lord rebuked him. Jesus recognized the authority of the government rulers and our need to submit to them.

Jesus knew that what was happening to him was the Father's plan and will. God could have easily prevented Jesus' arrest in the blink of an eye by sending mighty angel armies. Jesus went willingly to the cross for our sake. Isaiah 53 compares Jesus' quiet submission in this event to an innocent lamb being led to slaughter. Reflect on the Son of God's quiet submission to the Father's will for your sake.

*Lord, you went willingly to be condemned to death for my salvation. Thank you for the cross.*

# COMPASSION OF CHRIST

*When He saw the multitudes,*
*He was moved with compassion for them,*
*because they were weary and scattered,*
*like sheep having no shepherd.*
MATTHEW 9:36 NKJV

In Jesus' day, earthly rulers and religious teachers were in abundance. The Pharisees heaped burdens of rules and regulations on the people to the point where they felt hopeless of ever achieving right standing with God. The people were weary and spiritually worn from a lack of true spiritual leadership.

Since Jesus is fully God (Colossians 1:19), we can get a glimpse of the heart of God through him. When Jesus looks at people, he perceives their state of spiritual need. His heart is moved with compassion for those who need a deliverer. He sees beyond the external realities to the inner heart. Jesus doesn't just perform acts of compassionate love; he also feels compassion in his heart. We can learn from Jesus' example how to see and care for people beyond what is on the surface.

*Lord, thank you for your heart of compassion. Help me to see others around me the way you see them and to respond to any needs with action.*

# PAUL'S PRAYER

*I want you to understand what really matters,*
*so that you may live pure and blameless lives*
*until the day of Christ's return.*
PHILIPPIANS 1:10 NLT

Paul's prayer for the church at Philippi, to understand what really matters, is to have discernment about right and wrong, good and evil. This happens as we are increasingly transformed by God's work in us and changed into the people that he wants us to be. As Christ in us increases, we will desire what he desires. His priorities become our priorities.

To be pure and blameless does not mean we are sinless and perfect. Philippians 1:6 reminds us that God will complete the good work he began in us. Our perfection will only be fully realized in glory when Jesus returns. In the meantime, we no longer have an appetite for sin and run quickly to confess it when we stumble. According to verse 9, the basis of this discernment and blamelessness is love growing in our lives. Because of Christ's work in our hearts, we will increasingly love what he loves.

*Lord, may your transformation of my life be reflected in my priorities and in my love for others.*

# HOPEFUL COURAGE

*Wait for the LORD;*
*be strong, and let your heart take courage;*
*wait for the LORD!*
PSALM 27:14 NRSV

Fear comes naturally to us rather than courage. Fear is rash, impatient, and seemingly innate, as is indicated by the phrase "primal fear." Courage is something we have to strive to obtain. The ability to do something that scares us takes faith. The belief that we are doing what is right and necessary is what enables us to overcome our fear.

Waiting for God is to trust his ways rather than looking to our own resources. It is to have a confident expectation of God's ability to work. If we want to build our reliance on God, we ought to become more acquainted with how big God is. Rehearse the narratives of God's faithfulness to Noah, Joseph, Ruth, Daniel, and many others. Let your hope, trust, and courage spring from the boundless strength of the God we worship.

*Lord, I want to know your greatness. Help my courage grow and my fears fade in the light of who you are!*

# DILIGENT AND HUMBLE

*Be diligent in these matters;*
*give yourself wholly to them,*
*so that everyone may see your progress.*
1 TIMOTHY 4:15 NIV

Paul was Timothy's mentor in leading and teaching the faith community. Timothy was young, but Paul had confidence in his ability to teach others based on how God had gifted him. The phrase "so that everyone may see your progress" is not a contradiction of Matthew 6:1. Paul was exhorting Timothy to set forth an example to those he was leading. The goal was to encourage in others the same heart of devotion to God, and ultimately to bring him glory.

Being diligent means to work hard, to cultivate, and to be fully committed. This is no mere outward display of right behavior. We are to diligently guard the health of our own faith walk with God. Whether a teacher of many or an influencer of one, we are called to remain teachable and transparent. Avoid being puffed up with mere knowledge (1 Corinthians 8:1) and tend diligently to your heart. Be a living example of humble dependence on God.

*Lord, help my life and walk with you to be an encouragement to others and glorifying to you.*

# PRAYER AND PEACE

*Do not be anxious about anything, but in everything by prayer and supplication with thanksgiving let your requests be made known to God. And the peace of God, which surpasses all understanding, will guard your hearts and your minds in Christ Jesus.*

PHILIPPIANS 4:6-7 ESV

Prayer is the means by which we overcome our anxieties. 1 Peter 5:7 says we are to turn all our worries over to God because he cares for us. We are to approach God with the expectant faith that he will act (Hebrews 11:6), thanking him for what he is going to do. We don't know what the result will be, but God is in control and has our best interests at heart.

If we have truly released the burden of our anxieties and fears to the Lord, our hearts will be protected by the peace of God. His peace protects our minds from running to every possible scenario. It doesn't make sense that we should be at peace in the midst of distressing circumstances, so it could only be from God.

*Lord, when my heart is gripped with anxiety, help me to turn to you, asking and believing that you will act.*

# MARCH

You, O Lord, your mercy-seat love is limitless,

reaching higher than the highest heavens.

Your great faithfulness is so infinite,

stretching over the whole earth.

PSALM 36:5 TPT

# DOCTOR NEEDED

*Jesus answered them,*
*"It is not the healthy who need a doctor, but the sick.*
*I have not come to call the righteous, but sinners to repentance."*
LUKE 5:31-32 NIV

The Pharisees and religious teachers were critical of Jesus' behavior, namely that he was eating and spending time with tax collectors and sinners. A modern equivalent might be strippers and drug dealers. Jesus came to call those who know they are sinners to repentance. Not only that, but he provided the means to freedom from sin by laying down his very life.

Sometimes, we don't see ourselves the way Jesus does. We are just as sick at heart and in need of forgiveness as someone on death row. Maintaining an attitude of thankfulness keeps us aware of our dependence on God. Don't let your spiritual knowledge blind you to your desperate need for God. Ask him to show you what your true spiritual state is.

*Lord, help me to be conscious of my sin. Show me how much I need you.*

# FEAR NOT

*"Fear not, for I am with you;*
*be not dismayed, for I am your God;*
*I will strengthen you, I will help you,*
*I will uphold you with my righteous right hand."*
ISAIAH 41:10 ESV

The exhortation to not be afraid is repeated numerous times through the pages of Scripture. It is no surprise that God often has to remind us not to fear; it is so common to our experience as human beings. When we look at the circumstances around us, our hearts quickly give way to fear, anxiety, and imagining the worst.

The antidote to fear is God's very presence. In this one short verse, notice how many times God says, "I am," or "I will." He is here with all of his strength, help, and supporting grip. The perfect love that comes from God drives away fear, according to 1 John 4:18. God protects his own. Remember that you have been adopted as a child of the King.

*Father, thank you for adopting me as your beloved child through Jesus. Help me to not fear, but instead keep my eyes fixed on you.*

# ANSWERS TO PRAYER

*This is the confidence which we have before Him, that, if we ask anything according to His will, He hears us. And if we know that He hears us in whatever we ask, we know that we have the requests which we have asked from Him.*

1 JOHN 5:14-15 NASB

This verse and other similar ones do not mean we will get anything we pray for. The clarifying phrase "according to God's will" puts holes in that argument. According to James 4:3, often we don't receive what we ask for in prayer because we have self-serving motives.

Sometimes, we have no way of knowing what God's will is in a particular situation, and that's okay. We may ask to be healed from the flu, but we don't know if God's will is to heal us, or if he wants us to endure and trust him more through it. God's primary goal is to see our faith in him grow. Get to know God's will as it is expressed through the pages of Scripture. Then approach the Lord with confident faith.

*Lord, help me to have the right mindset when I come to you in prayer. I want to seek your will in all things.*

# MY FATHER'S HOUSE

*"There are many rooms in my Father's house;
I would not tell you this if it were not true.
I am going there to prepare a place for you."*
JOHN 14:2 NCV

Jesus said this to his disciples to comfort them after breaking the news that he was going away from them for a while. Although he was going to the cross, the resurrection was ahead. He was about to open the door to eternal life and the joy of being in heaven with him forever.

This description of the Father's house highlights how Jesus is like the heavenly bridegroom. In Jewish culture, an expectant groom would build an addition to his father's house. He would prepare new rooms, and after the wedding, bring his wife to live there with him. Jesus is painting a beautiful word picture of the loving relationship he has with all of his followers. We are the bride, and the nature of his love for us is complete commitment. What a comfort it is to know that this life is not all there is, and that we will be with the Lord forever in heaven.

*Lord Jesus, thank you for loving me and for the promise of eternal life in heaven with you.*

# UPHELD

*Though he fall, he shall not be cast headlong,*
*for the LORD upholds his hand.*

PSALM 37:24 ESV

This promise is for anyone who is God's follower. 2 Corinthians 4:8-9 says, "We are afflicted in every way, but not crushed; perplexed, but not driven to despair; persecuted, but not forsaken; struck down, but not destroyed" (ESV). Trials and difficulties are part of life and part of our Christian walk. The good news is that they serve to strengthen our faith, not destroy it. Nothing happens to us apart from God's sovereign will. He is the one who holds onto us and keeps us by his grace.

In our lives, God can take what may look like a defeating circumstance and use it to draw us closer to God than ever. We don't cherish the memory of difficult times in our lives, but when we look back on them, we can often recall the nearness and sweetness of God's presence. We can agree with Joseph that what was meant for evil, God intended for good (Genesis 50:20).

*Lord, use the difficulties in my life to produce good fruit.*
*Thank you that with you, the pain is not wasted.*

# ONE LOST SHEEP

*"What do you think? If a man owns a hundred sheep, and one of them wanders away, will he not leave the ninety-nine on the hills and go to look for the one that wandered off?"*

MATTHEW 18:12 NIV

Jesus is speaking to his disciples, making several comparisons in this passage to highlight the nature of his true followers. He compares his followers to sheep in the care of a shepherd. A sheep wandering off is a picture of us as sinners in need of rescue. The great hero of the story is the shepherd, who is the Lord. He is the one who pursues us no matter how far we have strayed in sin.

Jesus is pointing out that he came to save those who need a rescuer. He takes great joy in each person who recognizes his or her dependence on him. His mercy and compassion know no bounds. He does not sit back and wait for people to patch up their lives and then approach him. He moves toward us with fervency and initiative motivated by love.

*Lord, I need you. Thank you for coming to seek and to save the lost.*

# TRASH AND TREASURE

*I regard everything as loss because of the surpassing value of knowing Christ Jesus my Lord. For his sake I have suffered the loss of all things, and I regard them as rubbish, in order that I may gain Christ.*

PHILIPPIANS 3:8 NRSV

Before Paul met Christ, he put his confidence in his Jewish heritage, his religious zeal, and his ability to obey the rules. He used to believe that those things would score points with God and make him look good before other people. However, after he encountered the mercy and grace of God in the person of Jesus, everything changed.

For those of us who are in Christ, things that used to be worth living for no longer carry the same importance. We consider things like material wealth, personal achievement, and temporary pleasure to be as worthless as trash. We would renounce anything in our lives that tried to compete with Jesus being in first place in our lives. May our relationship with Jesus be so valuable to us that we count him as our greatest treasure.

*Lord, nothing else I could desire compares with you. Help me to live in a way that is consistent with that declaration.*

# SEEKING THE LORD

*"You will seek Me and find Me
when you search for Me with all your heart."*

JEREMIAH 29:13 NASB

Seeking God is a common theme in the Bible. To seek God is to set your mind and your heart on God (1 Chronicles 22:19). It is consciously focusing our attention on the Lord and overcoming obstacles in our own mind and heart that try to undermine that devotion. One of our greatest impediments to connection with God is our own pride. We must come to him in humility, recognizing our need for him.

We must seek God not because he is hard to find, but because we are fallible human beings. The great promise is that when we seek him in faith, our efforts will be rewarded (Hebrews 11:6). God delights in drawing us near and revealing himself to us. When we seek him, God promises that he will be found by us.

*Lord, help me to seek you with my whole heart and be satisfied in your presence.*

# TERMS OF ADOPTION

*The Father has loved us so much that we are called children of God.*
*And we really are his children. The reason the people in the world do*
*not know us is that they have not known him.*

1 JOHN 3:1 NCV

The greatness of the Father's love is nearly indescribable. The culminating purpose of his love for us—demonstrated through giving up his own Son—was to make us his own. We are not just called his children; we really are his.

We have been adopted to such an extent that we are co-heirs with Christ (Romans 8:16). The stipulation is that we will encounter suffering, just as Jesus himself endured suffering. Just as the world rejected Jesus, we will also encounter rejection for the sake of belonging to him. It is an honor to be counted worthy of suffering for Jesus. The good news is that persecution is temporary, and we will one day enter into glory with Jesus.

*Lord, thank you for adopting me into your family.*
*Help me to hold onto your promises when I encounter*
*mistreatment from others who reject you.*

# SOURCE OF HELP

*I lift up my eyes to the mountains—*
*where does my help come from?*
*My help comes from the LORD,*
*the Maker of heaven and earth.*
PSALM 121:1-2 NIV

This is one of the psalms of ascent, and it was likely sung as the people of Israel went up the hills to Jerusalem on feast days. The mountain of the Lord refers to the place of the center of worship. Many of the surrounding nations worshiped false gods on mountains or hills. However, the psalmist knew they couldn't put their confidence in false worship, but only in the Lord. He is the creator of all things, including every mountain; he is the only one worthy of our worship and our confidence.

We may have other false gods today, such as self-sufficiency, pride, or performance. None of these will prove faithful to us. Let us humbly come before God and seek him in the day of trouble. He is all-powerful, never changing, and his resources are unlimited. No matter how pressing our problems, God's grace is sufficient.

*Lord, you are the source of help, hope, and deliverance.*
*Help me to put my confidence in you alone.*

# PRAYER FOR PEACE

*May the Lord of peace himself
give you peace at all times in every way.
The Lord be with you all.*
2 THESSALONIANS 3:16 NIV

The church at Thessalonica was experiencing trouble, both from within and from outside the church. The people had become confused and afraid, and Paul wrote to exhort and encourage them. He prayed for peace to calm their fears. Not only that, but he prayed for God himself to be present with them.

The Lord of peace is Jesus himself, who made a way for us to be reconciled to God and one another through sacrificing his own life. Notice the repetition: all times, every way, and with you all. His peace is the answer in every circumstance, and for each person, no matter how far from God they may feel. He desires unity, not division in the church. We can see in other Scriptures that peace is something we are to pursue and fight for (Ephesians 4:3, James 3:18). Let us remain in the peace the Lord has provided.

*Lord, thank you for your presence and your peace. I want to uphold peace and unity in your church.*

# WEAKNESS

*My health may fail, and my spirit may grow weak,*
*but God remains the strength of my heart;*
*he is mine forever.*
PSALM 73:26 NLT

The psalmist is clearly voicing his discouragement. His bodily strength failing him is something we can identify with as fellow human beings. Our bodies suffer the effects of disease, age, and injury as we await the redemption of our bodies. We don't need to look far to find sadness, grief, and depression. Sometimes we feel completely spent, both physically and emotionally.

When we feel too weak to go on, we are in good company with the writers of the psalms. However, we don't have to throw up our hands and give up; sometimes we must fight for joy and hope. As believers, we have the best advocate in the midst of weakness. Psalm 23:3 says, "He restores my soul." Cling to the promise that absolutely nothing can separate you from God's love. Trust that in God's good timing and plan, he will bring you through.

*Lord, when I am at the end of myself, help me to trust that you are the strength of my heart.*

# GIVE MERCY

*"Give, and you will receive. You will be given much.
Pressed down, shaken together, and running over,
it will spill into your lap.
The way you give to others is the way God will give to you."*

LUKE 6:38 NCV

The preceding verse, Luke 6:37, brings clarity as to what kind of giving Jesus is speaking about: "Don't judge others, and you will not be judged. Don't accuse others of being guilty, and you will not be accused of being guilty. Forgive, and you will be forgiven." Jesus wants us to be merciful in our dealings with others because of how lavishly God has extended mercy to us. Rather than accusing others, he wants us to forgive.

Jesus goes on to illustrate how ridiculous it would be if someone tried to take a speck out of someone else's eye while a plank of wood was stuck in his or her own eye (Luke 6:41-42). Pride can blind us to our own sin and cloud our judgment. In humility, extend mercy generously in view of the mercy that God has for you.

*Lord, help me to be generous in mercy in the same way you have dealt mercifully with me.*

# BETWEEN A ROCK

*"The LORD will fight for you,*
*and you shall hold your peace."*
EXODUS 14:14 NKJV

God worked in miraculous ways to deliver the people of Israel. They had just been freed from slavery in Egypt, only to have Pharaoh and his troops come after them. They were trapped between the Egyptian army and the Red Sea. However, God did not abandon them. He was still leading them, but the people lost sight of all that and thought they were about to die. They only wanted back their old lives in slavery in Egypt.

Moses spoke words of assurance to the people, urging them to not be afraid. They didn't have to worry, because they were about to witness God's miraculous rescue at the parting of the sea. When circumstances look bleak, remember that it is God who fights for you. He alone receives the glory when we have no other hope of rescue than him. Trust that he will act on his promises.

*Lord, help me to keep my eyes on you rather than the problems I face. I know you can cause good to come from the worst circumstances.*

# FRUIT OF THE SPIRIT

*The fruit of the Spirit is love, joy, peace, forbearance,*
*kindness, goodness, faithfulness, gentleness and self-control.*
*Against such things there is no law.*
GALATIANS 5:22-23 NIV

Paul lists the evidence, or fruit, of the Holy Spirit's presence in our lives. Someone can identify where the Spirit is working by looking for these things, particularly in the context of how we treat others around us. In John 15, we can see that a spiritually fruitful life is one that is connected to Jesus. None of it is possible in our own strength; it is all because of the gift of God's grace to us.

We can use the list above as a spiritual health check-up. If we find our spiritual fruit is looking meager and shriveled, there is hope and help in the person of Jesus. We can turn to him and find refreshment and joy in coming back to him in repentance and trust. He delights in restoring you and takes joy in you.

*Lord, anytime I see these fruits in action, I am glimpsing your Spirit at work. Thank you for your grace!*

# GOD INTERVENED

*He saw that there was no one, he was appalled that there was
no one to intervene; so his own arm achieved salvation for him,
and his own righteousness sustained him.*

ISAIAH 59:16 NIV

Salvation is found in no one else. We are helpless without the
intervention of Jesus on our behalf. In Psalm 14, we are reminded
that there is no one who is righteous before God. Don't be misled
by the description of "he was appalled," as if God was shocked to
make the discovery that no one else was sufficient to step in. We
know that nothing takes God by surprise because he has infinite
knowledge. The phrasing emphasizes the fact that no one could
intercede but God alone.

Jesus came as God in human form to intercede and rescue us from
sin and its consequences. Just as a loving parent steps in to clean
up a toddler's mealtime mess, Jesus entered our world to lay down
his life; he rescued us from the stain of sin that we could never
wash away.

*Father, thank you for sending Jesus, your beloved Son,
to die for me.*

# PLEASING GOD

*Am I now seeking human approval, or God's approval?*
*Or am I trying to please people?*
*If I were still pleasing people,*
*I would not be a servant of Christ.*
GALATIANS 1:10 NRSV

Paul wrote this letter to the Galatians to correct them regarding a false, legalistic gospel that was infiltrating the church. He was so uncompromising in his defense of the true gospel that it led him to declare in verse 9, "If anyone proclaims to you a gospel contrary to what you received, let that one be accursed!" It's obvious from this bold declaration that Paul was not willing to sacrifice truth for the sake of currying favor with people.

Pleasing God often entails making other people unhappy, since God's will runs contrary to the world's agenda. Let us, too, make a bold stand in defense of the true gospel. Let us stand against any philosophy that would attempt to supplant the truth of salvation in Christ alone, by grace alone, through faith alone.

*Lord, the gospel is beautiful in its simplicity. Give me strength and wisdom to defend the gospel at any cost, including people's opinion of me.*

# ALL ABOUT HIM

*The LORD has made everything for its purpose,*
*even the wicked for the day of trouble.*
PROVERBS 16:4 ESV

Have you ever heard the saying "it's all about her" or "it's all about him?" It's not a favorable comment unless you are referring to our great and glorious God. With our Creator, it really is all about him, and it is all for him. Without him, nothing would exist at all.

In the midst of his perfect ways, there are things we don't understand. Hard things, sad things, tragic things, and yet we are assured by his Word that he is righteous in all that he does. We must trust by faith that his reasons for whatever he allows in this life were planned perfectly through his infinite wisdom for his purpose, his pleasure, and our good.

*You are almighty and powerful, God. Everything was made by you and for you. Help me to remember that no matter what may come, you already know the outcome. You are working all things together for my good so that it will please you and bring you glory.*

# CONSIDERED WORDS

*To watch over mouth and tongue
is to keep out of trouble.*
PROVERBS 21:23 NRSV

God has graciously given us the secret to staying out of trouble. Avoid having to pull that foot out of your mouth by simply thinking before you speak! Consider the motive of your words and the effect they will have before they exit your mouth.

A misspoken or careless word can literally break a heart, steal our sleep, and stick in our throats for days, months, or years. It has the power to destroy friendships, families, and careers. Ask the Holy Spirit to give you wisdom and self-control so that your mouth can be a conduit of his love and peace.

*God, thank you for your wise and protective instruction. I want my words to please you and encourage others. Keep me from speaking out of impure motives or haste. Make my words a symphony of love to all who hear them.*

# GREAT JOY

*I have no greater joy than this,*
*to hear that my children are walking in the truth.*
3 JOHN 1:4 NRSV

Teaching young children is a privilege, but it can be physically and emotionally exhausting. Some days feel like they will go on forever. You tire, wondering if the kids are listening to a word you say. Be assured that if you are training children in the Word, even when they are old, they will not depart from it.

What an immense joy to know if we are faithful to teach Scripture and lead children in the Lord's commands that in their later years, they will not abandon him. As we instruct them, lovingly discipline them, and guide their character, we will reap the benefit of peace, knowing that even if they do stray in life, God's promise will guide them back.

*Father, thank you for the privilege of teaching precious children about you. Help me to train them to be upright servants of the living God. Help them to grow in wisdom and desire relationship with you. Help me to be the example that leads them closer to you.*

# FAITH WINS

*By faith our ancestors received approval.*
HEBREWS 11:2 NRSV

Most people will go to extravagant extremes to win approval. Achieve more, learn more, do more, succeed more, over and over again in hopes of receiving the praise they desire. It's a never-ending, exhausting cycle of finding new ways to gain the applause of others.

Our spiritual forefathers had one step to receiving approval—faith. The patriarchs walked with God daily, nurturing a deep personal relationship with the Father. This closeness with the Father resulted in great faith which he counted as righteousness, and he was pleased by their unwavering trust. The only approval we need is from our Creator, and the way to win it is faith in him, pure and simple.

*Lord, I pray you will give me the gift of faith so that I may please you. I know that nothing I do can ever win your favor but if I trust in you, not in myself, I will receive approval from you. Thank you for the example of my spiritual ancestors. Help me walk with you and have a faith that never doubts.*

# LEARNING CONTENTMENT

*I am not saying this because I am in need,*
*for I have learned to be content whatever the circumstances.*
PHILIPPIANS 4:11 NIV

Ask yourself about that material possession, that relationship, or that position you desperately hunger for. Is it a need or a want? Picture yourself getting that all-important thing. Does it completely fulfill that voracious yearning, or does it soon pale? Now something else is needed to fill that hole.

Notice that the apostle Paul didn't just say be content; he said learn to be content. Contentment doesn't come naturally. It takes work to create a place in our hearts where our attitudes are not based on whether we have more than we need or are lacking. Regardless of our circumstances, we can always find contentment and peace in knowing God has promised to never leave us or forsake us.

*Father, when it comes down to it, you are all I really need. I am so thankful that you are Lord over all. Whatever I may need, you have promised, to provide for me, within your will. I know my peace lies in being content. Help me to commit to living fully satisfied with your presence in my life.*

# HELP GUARANTEED

*I asked the LORD for help, and he answered me.*
*He saved me from all that I feared.*
PSALM 34:4 NCV

Do you ever get so caught up in your fear that you feel you are panicking to find a way to eliminate it? You think of various scenarios for controlling what seems to be uncontrollable. You seek advice from people who claim to have the answers you are seeking, but none of them help.

And then a lightbulb comes on, and you consider prayer. We would all save a lot of time and heartache if we would believe the psalmist's testimony that God hears when we ask for help, and he answers. He alone has the perfect solution to anything that could be troubling us. When doubt comes, don't waste time; go to the only one who can listen and solve your deepest despair.

*God, when I get caught up in a frenzy of worry and attempt to find a solution on my own, please stop me in my tracks. Remind me of your loving desire to listen and answer my needs. I have but one place to go: your throne of grace, where I will find help and relief for all of life's circumstances.*

# OUR FATHER

*"Your kingdom come.*
*Your will be done,*
*On earth as it is in heaven."*
MATTHEW 6:10 NASB

The book of Revelation paints some spectacular pictures of a new heaven and a new earth—God's kingdom where Christ will reign forever, and we will rejoice and worship him. Jesus, knowing the glory of the coming kingdom, encouraged us in the Lord's prayer to petition for that day to arrive.

When this world passes away and God establishes our forever home with him, we will no longer have to pray for God's will. It will be the order of all things. No more sickness, no pain, no more tears. Rejoice in this future promise, knowing that when that day comes, our eternity will begin, and our joy will be complete.

*Our Father, who art in heaven, hallowed be thy name. Thy kingdom come, thy will be done, on earth as it is in heaven. Give us this day our daily bread. And forgive us our debts as we also have forgiven our debtors. And do not lead us into temptation but deliver us from evil. For thine is the kingdom, and the power, and the glory, forever.*

# OUR DELIVERER

*When the righteous cry for help, the LORD hears
and delivers them out of all their troubles.*

PSALM 34:17 ESV

We have been told that there are no guarantees in life, but for the children of God, there are. We have a promise from God that when we, who have been made righteous by the blood of Christ, call out to him, he hears, he answers, and he delivers. That is the absolute truth.

But what about that one time when it didn't look like he rescued you? Well, it didn't look like what you expected. It's because he knows and sees things that you can't. He has delivered you more times than you know this side of heaven. Trust and have faith in him. Everything he does is working together for good in your life.

*Lord, I know that your ways are higher than mine. When I cry out to you, I often have what I think is the perfect and only solution. I thank you for overruling me, so that you can give me your very best and deliver me in your wisdom and love.*

# REJOICE ALWAYS

*Rejoice in the Lord always;*
*again I will say, rejoice!*
PHILIPPIANS 4:4 NASB

Why should we rejoice? Because Jesus has conquered sin and death! As believers in him, we are assured that because of this, our sins are forgiven. We are redeemed, and we are sealed with the promise of the Holy Spirit. We did not choose Jesus, but he chose to die for us. God has lavished us with the riches of his grace. His plan is to help us thrive, growing us into the likeness of his Son. One day, we will live in his kingdom and be with him for eternity.

This is the reason we can and should rejoice, again, and again, and again!

*God, it overwhelms and humbles me when I think of all that you have done to save me. The fact that you chose me amazes me. I have every reason to rejoice consistently and to be eternally grateful for every great and wonderful gift you have bestowed on me. Thank you, Jesus.*

# MIND YOUR MOTIVES

*To set the mind on the flesh is death,*
*but to set the mind on the Spirit is life and peace.*
ROMANS 8:6 NRSV

What consumes your thoughts and drives your actions will speak volumes to you about your spiritual condition. How you feel after you have chosen to disobey God tells you where you are in your relationship with him. Do you feel remorse and repent, or do you justify your actions?

The Word tells us that if our hearts' motives follow the things of this world—getting ahead, acquiring all the toys, and self-fulfillment—then the sign at the end of the road is death. Living as a dwelling of the Holy Spirit and purposely choosing to please God brings life and peace. What does your mind reveal about your spiritual health today?

*Lord, I know from your Word that I am to take my captive thoughts to the throne of Christ, watch the intent of my heart, and guard my emotions. As a child of God, help me continually notice what I allow to enter my mind and how I react as that thought exits. Keep my mind set on your Spirit.*

# TIME IS TICKING

*"Repent of your sins and turn to God,
for the Kingdom of Heaven is near."*
MATTHEW 3:2 NLT

So many things in life are controlled by time constraints. The one-day sale or a work report with a delivery deadline. There are negative results and consequences if we don't act before the ticking clock runs out.

We live in a time of God's grace. Today, he invites all to come to him for the forgiveness of sins and freedom in Christ. But there is an end date for his offer. When Christ returns to reign over his kingdom and his judgment begins, time to repent will be lost. That is why we must share the good news with the world, for the kingdom of heaven could be much nearer than we think.

*Father, help me to live with urgency when it comes to sharing the gospel. Thank you for forgiving my sins and giving me the gift of salvation. Help me to notice the lost and dying every day and respond with boldness, telling them that they too, can repent, be forgiven, and live forever with you.*

# TEMPTATION OR TEST

*Let no one say when he is tempted, "I am tempted by God";*
*for God cannot be tempted by evil, nor does He Himself tempt anyone.*
JAMES 1:13 NKJV

According to its definition, temptation is a strong urge or desire to do wrong or evil. As the author of evil, Satan tries to trip us up daily by tempting us. Our Lord is holy and therefore does not tempt us, but he will test us. The definition of test is a procedure that determines the truth of something: in this case, the truth of our faith and commitment to God.

Next time you are tempted, remember who the source is, and whether you want to agree with evil. When a test comes, recognize that it is your good and loving heavenly Father developing a proven character of faith in you that is more precious than gold and will bring him glory.

*Lord God, please give me discernment to know the difference between a test and a temptation. I don't want to give in to the enemy's schemes against me. I desire to grow in faith and wisdom, allowing your tests to make me more into the image of your Son. I praise your goodness and your wise and wonderful ways in my life.*

# TRULY CHRISTLIKE

*Do not be conformed to this world, but be transformed by the
renewing of your minds, so that you may discern what is the will
of God—what is good and acceptable and perfect.*

ROMANS 12:2 NRSV

Have you ever met a Sunday Christian? They are someone who
appears to be saved at church on Sunday, but if you meet up with
them during the week, they are an entirely different person. They
are a chameleon of sorts, fitting and adapting to whatever way the
wind is blowing in our nonbelieving world, leaving behind a false
representation of what a true Christ follower is.

Scripture admonishes us to allow the Holy Spirit to renew our
minds, so that we can come into agreement with God's perfect will.
We have been given the mind of Christ, but it is up to us to submit,
listen to, and act on it. Only then will our actions be truly Christlike,
allowing the world to see who Jesus really is.

*Jesus, I am called to show your love to the world so that
others may be saved. Help me to stay closely connected
to you, and may I never misrepresent who I am in Christ.
Remind me to reject the fleeting ideals and desires of this
present world and revive my mind through your Holy Spirit.
Thank you for your will for my life.*

# REAL HUMILITY

*"Whoever exalts himself will be humbled,*
*and whoever humbles himself will be exalted."*
MATTHEW 23:12 ESV

So many see the word "humble" and think of it as negative. One dictionary says it is a state of being insufficient, but that is nowhere near Scripture's definition. In fact, humility showed up in the full sufficiency of Christ. When Jesus submitted to death on the cross in our place, he became the greatest of all by being the servant of all. For his obedience, he was exalted as King of kings and Lord of lords.

Our attitude should be the same as Jesus: humble servants who lovingly look to the needs of others ahead of our own. Serve with a pure heart and leave your exaltation up to God.

*Jesus, thank you for being the greatest servant of all and our perfect example. Thank you for your sacrifice of suffering that was rightfully mine. Help me not to think of myself, but instead to notice the needs of others. May I serve without thought of being honored and simply to please you.*

# APRIL

Your eyes saw my unformed body;

all the days ordained for me

were written in your book

before one of them came to be.

PSALM 139:16 NIV

# TRULY KNOWN

*Keep a good conscience so that in the thing in which you are slandered, those who disparage your good behavior in Christ will be put to shame.*

1 PETER 3:16 NASB

A conversation filters through the grapevine and makes its way to you. Someone made a derogative comment about your character or a statement about you that was an outright lie. It's a shock, and it stings. How should you react?

When you are confident in who you are in Christ and how your life reflects him, you don't need to react. You simply need to remember and reflect that you know the truth, and so does the one who matters most—Jesus. He knows your heart and your desire to live as he did. Rejoice in knowing that you are fully and truly known.

*Father, thank you that I can be confident in who I am and whose I am. Thank you for helping me pattern my life after yours so that when someone does speak falsehoods about me, I can remember the amazing work you have accomplished in me. I can also forgive because I am following your example. May others see Jesus in me today.*

# JOY IN THE JOURNEY

*LORD, I know that people's lives are not their own;*
*it is not for them to direct their steps.*
JEREMIAH 10:23 NIV

Like the road sign that warns of a wrong way, God's Word is the map for your life. When you start to go in a direction that is your choice, not his, you need to stop and remember that your life's course to abundance can only be steered by the Creator.

Our heavenly Father, who only gives good gifts to his children, can be trusted with every aspect of our time here on earth. Once we believe, submit, and have faith in his guidance, only then can we really rest in him and find joy in the journey.

*Father, I believe you know me and only want the best life for me. It a life that is lived knowing, loving, and following you. When I am tempted to take things into my own hands and drift away from your guidance, help me to remember that your ways are best. Thank you for lovingly planning my each and every step.*

# PERFECTION

*As for God, His way is perfect;*
*The word of the LORD is proven;*
*He is a shield to all who trust in Him.*

PSALM 18:30 NKJV

Perfection. It's unattainable. Still, we tend to strive for it more than we realize. We work hard to achieve something that matters and will last. What we accomplish may be good, beautiful, and meaningful, but it will never be absolutely perfect.

There is only one who is perfect—God. Everything he does is righteous. Every word he speaks is true. When we trust and have a firm belief in who he is and what he can do, we become confident in his perfect plan for us. Let's be thankful that we don't have to be perfect, because he is.

*Father, thank you for your love, which does not require that I achieve perfection. Thank you for calling me as your child to trust in you. You are magnificent God. I believe that you will always guide, protect me, and love me as my perfect heavenly Father.*

# HOPE JOY PEACE

*I pray that God, the source of hope,*
*will fill you completely with joy and peace*
*because you trust in him.*
*Then you will overflow with confident hope*
*through the power of the Holy Spirit.*

ROMANS 15:13 NLT

Can you remember a night when you were cooking dinner or reading a book and the electricity went out? Until the lines were filled with power again, there was not enough light or provision to accomplish what you were doing.

We all have times where we feel incapable, anxious, and discouraged. We try to build ourselves up, only to fall flat. That happens because we need the sufficiency of the Holy Spirit to help us. When we trust in his power to fill us, only then can we have the assurance of receiving complete hope, joy, and peace.

*Father, I desire hope, joy and peace that I can depend on. Please help me to trust in the power of the Holy Spirit in my life. You can provide in a way that is constant and beyond my comprehension.*

# REAPING A REWARD

*The reward for humility and fear of the LORD
is riches and honor and life.*
PROVERBS 22:4 ESV

Words and emotions like humility or fear don't usually cause us to think of anything positive. But in God's lexicon, they are words of life. True humility is not a sense of unworthiness, but rather a recognition of your worth to God. Fear is having reverence and awe of God, not being afraid. The Bible also calls fear the beginning of wisdom.

As God calls us to submit to him in humility and fear, we reap the benefits. We are assured that we will be blessed with abundance in a life of walking with our Lord. He is worthy. Our worthiness is due to the sacrifice of our Savior, and in his goodness, we receive the reward.

*I am so amazed by your goodness, Father. I submit myself in humility before you. You deserve my awe and respect. Help me daily to come to you with attitudes that please you.*

# MOUNTAIN MOVER

*Every valley shall be raised up,*
*every mountain and hill made low;*
*the rough ground shall become level,*
*the rugged places a plain.*

ISAIAH 40:4 NIV

There is no way out. Ever feel that way? Life can present us with ways that seem like dead ends, capable of opening up only if there is some type of supernatural intervention. We confess we need a miracle.

Thankfully, we have a miracle worker, and he is always working on our behalf in unseen places. He sees everything that we are going through. He is capable of moving our mountains, parting our seas, and eventually, bringing us into eternity, where he has prepared a place for us. Nothing is impossible with our God.

*Father, sometimes I hit a wall and there appears to be no solution. Then I remember that I serve a God of limitless power. Remind me to come to you immediately in faith and expectation of what you will do.*

# TRANSFORMED BY RENEWAL

*Let the Spirit renew your*
*thoughts and attitudes.*
EPHESIANS 4:23 NLT

We are bombarded daily with messages, texts, and social media comments. When we read the news on the disturbing conditions of our world, or view posts that cause us to believe the grass is greener on the other side, it can negatively alter our mood. When this infects us, it also affects our family, friends, and work environment.

God's provision for this situation is his Holy Spirit. When we get alone with God in prayer, letting his Spirit dwell within us, quiet us, and soothe us, our outlook and demeanor change. We start to adopt God's perspective. Let him transform your mind to come into agreement with his Holy Spirit.

*Father, I admit that my focus on our digital community can cause me to think everyone's life is better than mine. Help me to take my eyes off of the latest posts and cast my vision on you. Help me to be an example to my family, friends, and co-workers of a Christ follower, not a social media seeker.*

# SPIRITUAL GIFTS

*Since we have gifts that differ according to the grace given to us, each of us is to use them properly.*
ROMANS 12:6 NASB

Don't we all love receiving gifts? Especially ones that have been chosen with extra care and thought to individually suit us. We enjoy giving gifts as well. However, how would we feel if we knew that the gift we had given was not used at all, but sitting on a closet shelf in the dark?

God carefully considered the spiritual gifts he gave to all his children. His gifts are free, but they come with his heart's desire for us to use them. We are the body of Christ, and when each of us incorporate our gifts into our daily lives, we fulfill God's purpose for our life and the church and bless others in the process.

*Thank you, Father, for thinking so carefully about me as you chose the gifts and talents you bestowed on me. I don't want to miss a single minute using these for your glory. Please help me be mindful of their purpose in your kingdom and to apply them daily.*

# WISE CHOICES

*If any of you is lacking in wisdom, ask God,*
*who gives to all generously and ungrudgingly,*
*and it will be given you.*
JAMES 1:5 NRSV

Decisions can be incredibly difficult, especially if they have long term repercussions. We consider the pros and cons. We toss and turn at night with the "what if's" of making the wrong choice. We want the confidence to know we are using excellent judgment, knowledge, and insight.

God graciously offers us his gift of wisdom in great measure. If we ask in faith, we can believe he will deliver. We can be assured, as we prayerfully consider any situation we face, that God will lead us and enable us to act with good judgment and understanding.

*Father, you desire me to seek wisdom, and you promise that if I believe, I will receive it. I want to please you by being prudent in all my decisions. Help me to have the mind of Christ in all that I say and do.*

# SPIRITUAL AUTHORITY

*Obey your leaders and act under their authority. They are watching over you, because they are responsible for your souls. Obey them so that they will do this work with joy, not sadness. It will not help you to make their work hard.*

HEBREWS 13:17 NCV

We are required to follow the laws enacted by our government, else there can be dire consequences. In the same way, we need to listen to those God has placed in spiritual positions. Godly spiritual leaders speak the truth of the Word in the form of pastors, mentors, and ministry leaders. They are placed in our lives to guide, teach, and train us. Our lives are better when we obey their teaching.

We encourage those in authority when we joyfully follow their instruction and speak our appreciation. If you haven't told your pastor lately how grateful you are for their work, consider doing it soon. Your kind words will bless your leader and please God.

*Father, thank you so much for blessing me with spiritual leaders to guide me into a mature relationship in Christ. I pray you will encourage them and fill them with joy. Help me to obey the living Word that they preach to me and help them know how pleased you are with them today.*

# SPIRITUAL ATHLETES

*We have all of these great witnesses who encircle us like clouds. So we must let go of every wound that has pierced us and the sin we so easily fall into. Then we will be able to run life's marathon race with passion and determination, for the path has been already marked out before us.*

HEBREWS 12:1 TPT

Did you know that you are destined to be a spiritual athlete? God has determined our path, and he asks us to enter the race of service with wholehearted dedication. Spiritual athletes who want to run the race well for God must throw off the hinderances of sin in order to serve to their best ability.

Through the Old Testament we can witness our spiritual family's faith in action, their race well run. The Bible tells us that David, when he had served God's purpose in his generation, fell asleep. As David did, let's run the race by finishing the work God has purposed for us. Then we will win the reward of hearing God say, "Well done, good and faithful servant."

*Father, when I sin, help me confess and repent. Show me any hidden sin. I don't want anything to hinder me from fulfilling the purpose you have given me. Help me to run well until the day I have served my purpose and enter into your presence.*

# TIMES AND PLACES

*Come now, you who say, "Today or tomorrow we will go to such and such a town and spend a year there, doing business and making money." Yet you do not even know what tomorrow will bring. What is your life? For you are a mist that appears for a little while and then vanishes. Instead you ought to say, "If the LORD wishes, we will live and do this or that."*

JAMES 4:13-15 NRSV

We serve a good Father who wants to give us his very best. He has a specific intent for our life. He has ordained the times and places we live. When we step out without praying for his guidance, we might find ourselves in opposition to his will. We are wise when we wait to hear from the Lord on the direction we should take.

Life here is short. While we are here, our goal should be to follow and obey the Lord in all that we do. Let's all hold our lives with an open hand before the Lord, always putting his desires ahead of our own.

*Father, I am thankful for your good purpose and plan for my life. I don't want to spend time doing anything that is outside of your will. I pray that my life here will be a testimony to who you are and your love for all mankind.*

# EXPRESSION OF LOVE

*No one has ever seen God.*
*But if we love each other, God lives in us,*
*and his love is brought to full expression in us.*
1 JOHN 4:12 NLT

Our world is so desperate for love. If we want to change the course of mankind and show humanity the exorbitant love of God, we must love one another. No one can see God, but when we invite Christ into our hearts as our Savior, his Holy Spirit enters us and transforms us. This transformation makes it possible for Jesus to love others through us, and they in turn see him.

To carry the love of God to others is a great privilege. Let us all express the greatest gift of all by generously giving love to everyone that we encounter daily.

*Father, I am so privileged to be a conduit of your love. Help me spread joy, kindness, and most of all, your love to everyone I encounter. When people look at me or engage with me, let them not see me, but let them see you.*

# EXTRAVAGANT PLANS

*"For I know the plans I have for you," declares the LORD,*
*"plans to prosper you and not to harm you,*
*plans to give you hope and a future."*
JEREMIAH 29:11 NIV

When you consider that the God of the universe has plans specifically for you, do you feel a sense of amazement? He is a compassionate, kind, gracious, generous God. Every intention he has for us is purposeful and for our good, even if it doesn't look good right away. God is doing a great work in us. It is not to hurt us but to encourage us, provide for us, and give us his abundance.

Look forward today with hopeful expectation and faith that God is doing his best on your behalf. We can live, knowing that we will experience spiritual prosperity, because we serve a good God.

*Father, what joy, what rest, in knowing that you gave great thought and moved with a heart of love when you prepared your plan for me. Make my ears attentive to your voice and give me great faith to carry out the course you have laid out for me. Thank you for the future you have in store for me.*

# COVETOUSNESS

*Wrath is fierce and anger is a flood,*
*But who can stand before jealousy?*
PROVERBS 27:4 NASB

No one likes to be confronted with anger or wrath, but the green-eyed monster is one of the worst villains we can encounter. We don't have to go far to meet up with jealousy because it can reside in our own hearts. When it does, it eats us up, steals our sleep, and causes us to withhold love from others. And when others are jealous of us, it can cause a great divide and even destroy a relationship.

The Holy Spirit wants to instill his fruit in us. Covetousness should never be part of our character. We have been transformed by Christ and empowered by his Spirit. Let us live a life of love, humility, and gratitude for the life God has given us.

*Jesus, when jealousy rears its ugly head in me, please convict me with your Holy Spirit. I know being jealous doesn't change anything, but it can hurt everyone around me. Help me instead to be happy for other's successes, looking to you alone for favor in my life.*

# ENEMIES NO MORE

*If while we were enemies we were reconciled to God by the death of his Son, much more, now that we are reconciled, shall we be saved by his life.*
ROMANS 5:10 ESV

It's hard to think of yourself as an enemy, hostile and in opposition to God, but at one time, we were all in that condition. How great is the grace that God freely bestows on us once we become believers in Jesus! All enmity is gone; we are beloved, forgiven, and sealed for eternity with his Holy Spirit.

We did nothing to deserve or earn his provision for our salvation, and it cost him everything. Jesus went to the cross of his own free will to secure our salvation and eternal security. He lives today to keep and sanctify us. What a glorious Savior.

*Jesus, when I consider your incredible sacrifice, it amazes me. When I realize I was your enemy when you made that sacrifice, it humbles me. Knowing that you live to continue doing your good work in my life makes me want to surrender to you completely. I am thankful for your great love, which ensures that we will live in eternity together, forever.*

# PURPOSEFUL PAIN

*"I will not cause pain
without allowing something new to be born," says the LORD.
"If I cause you the pain, I will not stop you from giving birth
to your new nation," says your God.*

ISAIAH 66:9 NCV

When we experience pain, we can't be certain when it will subside or what the final outcome will be. When God allows pain, he promises that it will accomplish his good purpose in his perfect timing. We can trust that he is working for us and that during the dark night of our soul, he is in control. Our hardship might be excruciating, but if we endure and have faith, there will be benefit, insight, and growth; something new will spring from it.

Take heart, have faith, and trust in God with the hopeful expectation that once you have persevered, he will birth great things in you for his glory.

*Father, I don't like pain. I desperately want it to leave as soon as it arrives. But because I know who you are and that your ways are perfect, I will trust in you. Hold me under the shadow of your wing. I know you will bring me through. There will be a transformation that makes it all worth it and glorifies you in the process.*

# OUR DEFENDER

*"The LORD your God is the one who goes with you
to fight for you against your enemies to give you victory."*
DEUTERONOMY 20:4 NIV

Do you ever have the feeling that someone is following you?
You turn to look, but there is no one there. As believers we have
an enemy, Satan. He is always looking for ways to kill, steal, and
destroy. We may not be able to see him, but he is persistent,
thoroughly evil and active in his pursuit. We must not let our guard
down, and instead fight back with the armor of God.

The good news about this spiritual battle is that Satan loses, and
we win! Jesus secured that victory for us on the cross, and it is
done. So, take authority and tell the devil to flee. You are a child of
God, protected and sealed in him.

*Thank you, Jesus, for defeating the grave and sentencing
the devil when you died and rose again. He can launch his
arrows, but they have no impact because of your power,
which is far greater. I have nothing to fear, for I serve a
faithful, all-powerful God who will always defeat my enemy.*

# WIN OR LOSE

*"What does it profit them if they gain the whole world,
but lose or forfeit themselves?"*
LUKE 9:25 NRSV

What do you want in this life? Some strive for money, fame, and influence. Others want love, family, and friends. Whatever you want to achieve or gain, what matters most is the motive behind your goal. Beware of trying to make your mark in this world by self-promoting, self- serving means.

People who live only for this life will be, at their end, tragically surprised that they missed the whole point. They may have momentary success on earth, but they lose themselves in the process. Make no mistake; life is short, and we get one shot at it. A life lived in surrender to Christ is one that has truly found its purpose, treasure, and everlasting security.

*Jesus, help me to build my treasure in heaven, not on this earth. I want to serve and love well here so that others will be drawn to you. Please, help me live with an eternal goal in mind, seeking not my will but yours alone.*

# GOD'S GUIDELINES

*"You will prosper, if you take care to fulfill the statutes and judgments with which the LORD charged Moses concerning Israel. Be strong and of good courage; do not fear nor be dismayed."*

1 CHRONICLES 22:13 NKJV

Have you ever noticed that an outcome is so much better when you do things the right way? When our motives are pure and our actions virtuous, we know that God will allow our lives to prosper. If you are in doubt of the hidden motive of your heart, ask Jesus, and he will be faithful to reveal anything that is not of him.

As believers, we have the righteousness of Christ. With Christ in us, there is no reason for fear, lack of faith, absence of courage, or discouragement. We must obey God and regularly examine our hearts to remove any wrong intentions. Only then can we trust that it will lead to spiritual success and a life that looks more like Jesus' life.

*Father, thank you so much for giving me your guidelines for a life that prospers. I am grateful for the knowledge that no weapon formed against me will stand, and that there is no reason for fear or to be disillusioned. Help me to follow your commands and fulfill your purpose for my life.*

# PASSING DESIRES

*This world and its desires are in the process of passing away,*
*but those who love to do the will of God live forever.*
1 John 2:17 TPT

Have you ever wanted an item so much that your desire couldn't be quenched until you got it? When you finally acquired what you had craved, you felt a surge of fulfillment. But once you got it home and lived with it for a while, eventually it didn't quite satisfy how you had envisioned. It lost its luster, and the momentary gratification quickly subsided.

Nothing we attain in this life will bring us lasting joy. When our priority is to do God's will and share Jesus with others, we can look forward to eternal elation. The reality is that this world will pass away, and the best is yet to come. It will be absolute perfection!

*Jesus, the only thing I can take from this world to my home with you are other souls I have led to you. Help me to be bold and to joyfully share the good news. Thank you that someday, we who know and love you will live with you forever in your kingdom.*

# ULTIMATE AUTHORITY

*"With God are wisdom and might;*
*he has counsel and understanding."*
JOB 12:13 ESV

Some people pursue strange and unusual sources for advice, from psychics to online social media forums. There are those who only seek out individuals they know will agree with their choice, in order to justify the decision they have already made.

We serve the one true God, who is the source of all intelligence and who is all-powerful. He stands ready to advise us and give us his knowledge on all situations we face in life. Let's make sure we always go first in prayer to the ultimate authority for guidance and instruction.

*Father, I praise you for your wisdom, your power, and your desire to instruct and guide me. When I need counsel, help me to always go first to you in prayer before I seek advisement elsewhere. Thank you for holding all of the answers for all of my needs.*

# SHOWING GOD'S LOVE

*Pursue peace with everyone,*
*and the holiness without which no one will see the Lord.*
HEBREWS 12:14 NRSV

Jesus left us explicit instructions before he ascended. We are to go out into the world and make disciples of all nations. How do we do that with all the dissension in the world, the vast disagreements, the social separation?

We can only show God's love to the world if we are agents of peace, actively pursuing unity with all we encounter. We are the conduit through which the Holy Spirit is visible. We must have a goal of holiness, which only comes by nurturing a consistent relationship with Jesus. Then Christ will be seen through us, and others will see him, receive him, and become his disciples.

*Father, you tell us to be holy as you are holy. Help me to be filled with your holiness as I come to you daily, read your Word, and pray to you. Then, help me to go out into the world and spread your love, exhibit your peace, and lead others to you.*

# SACRIFICIAL PERSEVERANCE

*I also persevered in the work on this wall, and we acquired no land,
and all my servants were gathered there for the work.*

NEHEMIAH 5:16 ESV

We all want to work alongside an authority figure that is fair,
trustworthy, considerate, and humble. As governor in the land of
Judah, Nehemiah was such a man. He feared God, so he made sure
that the people's welfare was his number one priority. He sacrificed
his own financial benefits, wanting what was best for those he
served.

We serve the ultimate supernatural authority. God, who is wise,
honest, loving, and good, only wants what is best for us. He
persevered in finding a solution for our sin through the sacrifice of
his Son, Jesus, and freely granted us forgiveness. It's the greatest
gift, and it's ours if we will accept it. If you haven't yet, won't you do
so today?

*Jesus, thank you for dying on the cross for me. I
remember how grateful I felt the day I asked you into my
heart and knew you had forgiven all of my sins. I trust you
every day of my life as my Lord and Savior. Help me share
you with others, so they can be forgiven and know your love.*

# A LOVING COMMANDMENT

*"This is My commandment,
that you love one another,
just as I have loved you."*
JOHN 15:12 NASB

A good commanding officer expects their soldiers to obey with exacting precision. Not doing so could bring them and others great harm. Their directives are given to achieve the best outcome.

Our good and wise God instructs us to consider others' needs above our own and to love one another above all. When we act in an absence of love, it can render our witness ineffective. God charges us to love because he wants everyone to come to salvation. Let's submit to his command, so that the world will recognize Jesus in us and come to know him.

*I desire to have your heart of love, Jesus. I know that I don't always love others, and I ask forgiveness for times I may have caused pain by not offering my love. Let me care for others, so that they see your love and come to know you as their Lord and Savior.*

# HEAVENLY HOME

*One thing I ask from the Lord, this only do I seek:*
*that I may dwell in the house of the Lord all the days of my life,*
*to gaze on the beauty of the Lord and to seek him in his temple.*

PSALM 27:4 NIV

At some point, most of us have envisioned our dream house. We would construct it to our heart's desire, and when finished, fill it with our favorite décor, friends, family, and wonderful memories.

As believers, we have a longing for a home that cannot be fulfilled in this world. Our true citizenship is in heaven, where God has prepared for us a place of unimaginable beauty. And best of all, he is there, and he wants us to be there with him. In our magnificent heavenly home, as we view his glory daily, we will worship and adore him all the days of our eternal life.

*Lord, I can't even begin to imagine the beauty you have in store for me in heaven. I know my eyes will be locked in elation on the magnificent sights you have created for those who love you. While I live on this earth, I will seek you, but I will look forward to the day when I will always gaze on you.*

# ALL WE NEED

*They will not be disgraced in hard times;*
*even in famine they will have more than enough.*
PSALM 37:19 NLT

Our faith is stretched when we experience difficult seasons. Jesus alerted us that hardships will befall us all, saying that in this world we would have trouble, but to take heart, for he has overcome the world (John 16:33). Regardless of what crises you may face, you can be confident that God is with you and for you.

Therefore, we have no reason to admonish God. At times, we might feel like we have a target on our backs, but God's power dispels the arrows of the enemy. Wearing our spiritual battle gear enables us to be conquerors in Christ, giving us all that we need to be victorious.

*Jesus, thank you for going before me. You provided the sacrifice, prepared the way, and planned my steps. You have given me your promise that you will never leave me or forsake me. I know whatever I face, you are there in the midst of it with me, and you will be faithful to bring me through to the other side. There, I will see your purpose and the victory!*

# HE LISTENS

*"Then you will call upon Me and go and pray to Me,*
*and I will listen to you."*
JEREMIAH 29:12 NKJV

Have you ever tried to hold a conversation with a friend or a spouse and realized that they have not listened to a word you said? Frustrating, isn't it? You might try to talk louder, or even say something silly, alarming, or non-sensical to get their attention.

We can be thankful that God promises that when we come to talk to him, he will listen. We never have to work to get his interest; he is always ready and eager to hear from his children. Knowing that he invites us, it is an offer we shouldn't and can't refuse. Don't waste this privilege; call on him today.

*Dear Father, I am so grateful that you ask me, your child, to call upon you. I have assurance that when I cry out to you, I am heard by you. Thank you for never tiring of listening to me. I can expect your wise answer in your perfect timing.*

# FOR A PURPOSE

*My brothers and sisters, whenever you face trials of any kind, consider it nothing but joy, because you know that the testing of your faith produces endurance; and let endurance have its full effect, so that you may be mature and complete, lacking in nothing.*

JAMES 1:2-4 NRSV

Anything of value usually comes with some difficulty. Giving birth can be excruciatingly painful, but once a mother has endured the pain, a new life is born. The discomfort is suddenly forgotten. Delight in the baby takes precedence.

When God allows a trial in our life, we can be confident he is working something in our lives for good. God wants us to have faith and to learn patience, and from that patience develop an attitude of joy. God desires that his children lack nothing. We must believe everything God allows in our lives is for us, not against us. In times of trial, trust him, and soon you will experience joy and become who God intended you to be.

*Father, I am so grateful that you don't leave me as I am. Your perfect desire is for me to mature. I understand that my growth will necessitate trials, but I know your will for me was designed out of goodness and love. Help me keep my eyes on you, knowing that when I come out the other side, I will be more like Jesus.*

# EVER PRESENT

*"Where two or three are gathered in my name,*
*there am I among them."*
MATTHEW 18:20 ESV

There is power in prayer. As we join with others to approach the throne of grace, God promises his presence. Scripture also admonishes us not to neglect meeting together, and when we do, to encourage one another. What a privilege it is to gather to worship, pray, serve, and enjoy each other's company while knowing Jesus is in our midst.

There is also assurance in the Word that when we seek God as individuals, we will find him. He is ever present with us and loves to spend time alone with each of us. The time we spend with God as individuals is crucial to our walk with him. We need to remember that the only way to truly know our Lord is to meet one-on-one with him consistently.

*Lord, as Creator of all and Lord over all, you desire to meet with each of us, whether that is in a group or individually. Help me to be mindful to never neglect praying and meeting with other believers. Help me to start this habit today, remaining constant in my individual pursuit of knowing you.*

# MAY

Your faith and love rise within you as you access all the treasures of your inheritance stored up in the heavenly realm. For the revelation of the true gospel is as real today as the day you first heard of our glorious hope, now that you have believed in the truth of the gospel.

COLOSSIANS 1:5 TPT

# HOPE ON THE HORIZON

*Certainly there is a future,*
*And your hope will not be cut off.*
PROVERBS 23:18 NASB

The Lord is eternal, and so are his promises. Our hope is not in vain. Those who put their hope in earthly treasures and temporary gains will face bitter disappointment one day, for their hope will surely be cut off.

That is why, above all else, we must hope in the Lord. He has offered us a plethora of promises if we choose to trust and follow him. He will provide a way for us so that we may always choose to walk in righteousness. His path may not be the easiest one to walk, but it is the only path that leads to an eternal future.

*God, renew my hope and help me follow you wherever you may lead. More than any merits or gains here on earth, I want a true and lasting relationship with you. Thank you for your promise of a future. I know that my hope will not be cut off, and I will not be disappointed.*

# FOUNDATIONAL FREEDOM

*We have freedom now, because Christ made us free. So stand strong.
Do not change and go back into the slavery of the law.*
GALATIANS 5:1 NCV

It was by way of a truly great sacrifice that we were granted
freedom from the bondage of sin. We were slaves to a law that
we were incapable of upholding, but Christ set us free by paying
for our sins himself. Through his death on the cross, we now live
guiltless.

Do not take hold of the guilt that was paid for at such high a cost!
All has been forgiven by him, and that is the foundation of our
freedom. We were made righteous, not by our own actions, but
by the actions of our Savior, who fulfilled the law and conquered
death forever.

*Help me, Father, to remember that it is by your grace
and sacrifice alone that I am free. My good deeds are not
payment for sin. They are an expression of my love and
gratitude to you for what you have done for me.*

# BROTHER'S KEEPER

*"The foreigner residing among you
must be treated as your native-born.
Love them as yourself, for you were foreigners in Egypt.
I am the LORD your God."*

LEVITICUS 19:34 NIV

Just because someone looks different, speaks another language, or is from somewhere far away does not mean they are any less deserving of our love and hospitality. As members of the body of Christ, our allegiance is first and foremost to the Most High. Therefore, it is our duty and our delight to love sisters and strangers alike and treat them with welcoming love.

One day, the tables could turn. We may find ourselves in a foreign land, feeling out of place. Since we are all under the same God and each created in his image, ethnicity and culture should not dictate the reach of our love.

*Open my eyes, dear Father, to recognize foreigners around me who may need a welcoming gesture or embrace. Please, keep me from becoming closed off from or even intimidated by people or behaviors different than what I am accustomed to. Remind me that we are all your children, beloved by you.*

# BLESSED ARE YOU

*"Blessed are those who are persecuted for righteousness' sake,
for theirs is the kingdom of heaven."*
MATTHEW 5:10 NKJV

One of the strongest and most obvious testimonies we have is that Christ has redeemed us and filled us with himself. From this comes our dauntless joy under terrible circumstances. When our faith is tested and put under pressure, that is when it becomes clear how real and unbreakable it truly is.

We all have bad days. We all fail and act foolishly. In the moments that matter, however, Christ's joy will shine through a Christian in such a way that his presence and power will be undeniable. It is not by our strength, determination, or courage; it is by our faith in the promise that God will uphold his children, no matter what.

*Lord, in every trial, temptation, and struggle, please walk with me moment by moment. I am not strong enough on my own, but that is the point. You are strong enough. When the dark times hit, others will recognize the God that I serve, because they will see me leaning on you and making it through.*

# PEACE IN STRONGHOLDS

*"Peace be within your walls,
and security within your towers."*
PSALM 122:7 NRSV

The children of God are so easily made combative. It's as if we are afraid that if we don't complain, we'll be neglected or trodden down. This opposes the truth that "blessed are the humble, for they will inherit the earth" (Matthew 5:5). In the same way, the peaceful will not be downtrodden easily. Their faith does not make them less secure, because as today's psalm points out, there is protection within their fortresses.

We can't forget where the Christian's peace resides: inside walls and fortresses. The sound truth and faith of Christ are our stronghold from which we view the world around us. It is secure enough for us to be at peace, though the war continues. We are soldiers walking in assurance, alert yet consoled, opposed yet gracious.

*My Rock and Defender, how great is your goodness to me. You seek my peace and security in the midst of troubling circumstances. You provide me with your Word, which is applicable, unchanging, and unbreakably true. May it forever be my fortress.*

# AT THE HEART

*"Don't judge by his appearance or height, for I have rejected him.*
*The Lord doesn't see things the way you see them.*
*People judge by outward appearance, but the Lord looks at the heart."*
1 SAMUEL 16:7 NLT

Rather than worry too much about our physical attractiveness or our reputations, we ought to be fostering a beautiful and godly heart. Similarly, before making rash judgments about others based on appearance or hearsay, let's take the time to understand others for who they really are.

We have not all come from the same starting point, and we each have unique journeys. The Lord cares about our hearts. Since only he can see a person's heart, we should listen to him and refrain from judging others.

*Almighty God, teach me to care about the things you care about and see things the way you see them. I want to be pleasing to you far more than I desire the approval of others. Soften my heart and help me love others the way you do, with understanding and without condemnation.*

# COMPASSION

*Keep being compassionate*
*to those who still have doubts.*
JUDE 1:22 TPT

Doubt is not a disappointment to the Lord; he is our Rock for a reason. He knows that we will have doubts. We will fail, we will disobey, and we will wander. He is our immovable Rock so that we have something to hang on to and to trust when we cannot trust ourselves.

When others experience doubts and are brave enough to voice them, rather than become uneasy or condemning, let's show them compassion by walking with them through their journey for answers. Remember the way the Lord showed us compassion and offered us answers. God is bigger than our doubts. He is compassionate and long-suffering on our behalf.

*Oh Lord, I am so weak, and my faith feels so small at times. Over and over throughout the Scriptures, you have shown me what you can do with broken people and very little faith, and I ask that you use me in the same way for your glory. Help me not to be intimidated by the doubts and questions of others, but to look to you for truth and answers. You are the Rock.*

# NEVER ALONE

*Even though I walk through the valley of the shadow of death,*
*I fear no evil, for You are with me;*
*Your rod and Your staff, they comfort me.*
PSALM 23:4 NASB

Even when we walk through the bleakest seasons, we can be fearless and resolute by keeping our eyes on Jesus. Don't become distracted or discouraged by the darkness around you, for darkness always gives way to daybreak.

Although the sin and evil around us may seem more powerful than we are, we need to remember that we are never alone. God is on our side, and he already has gained victory over darkness. With our eyes on him and our minds made up, he will lead us through the valley and to the top of the mountain.

*When I am gripped with fear, Lord, I will cling to your promises. When my sorrow seems too big, I will remember that you are bigger. The reign of sin and darkness will one day be swallowed up. Even now, they cannot overcome me. You are with me always.*

# INFALLIBLE WORD

*All Scripture is given by inspiration of God, and is profitable for doctrine, for reproof, for correction, for instruction in righteousness.*
2 TIMOTHY 3:16 NKJV

The Bible is not simply a self-help book to supplement our desired lifestyles. God's Holy Scriptures are the guidelines for our lives. They were inspired by our loving Father, inscribed for us so that we may know the right way to live. They are our living hope, as they tell the testimony of Jesus Christ.

It can be tempting to succumb to the habit of reading the Bible purely out of discipline and for the sake of our moral checklist. But when we open our hearts to truly receive its wisdom, we will be moved by its timeless truths. Its words hold the power to transform our lives and guide us into the fullness of life which God intended.

*Father God, thank you for your Word. It brings life and hope. I open its pages expectantly, eager to learn because you are the greatest teacher, and I yearn for your truth.*

# BE ALIVE

*"Love the LORD your God with all your heart,*
*all your soul, and all your strength."*

DEUTERONOMY 6:5 NCV

God doesn't want us to live apathetically. Even though his plan is for him to be brought all the glory that he is due, he has decided to not accomplish this without exalting us, as well. When God commands us, "Love the Lord your God with all your heart, all your soul, and all your strength," he is proclaiming to us how we can flourish. This, he says, is the only way to be alive. There is no other path to flourishing.

How blessed we are to have a Savior and Lord who will be served simply by our walk in the path of life! He throws down every burden from our conscience and commands us to love him in every way, with all that we have.

*Lord, you are clothed in majesty and surrounded by mercy. Your kindness knows no limit and your glory is forever visible. Teach me to love you in everything I do, in measureless devotion to the one who died for my salvation.*

# HE UNDERSTANDS

*We do not have a high priest who is unable to empathize with our weaknesses, but we have one who has been tempted in every way, just as we are—yet he did not sin.*

HEBREWS 4:15 NIV

Ours is a God who sees us. He is not a distant, uncaring deity, but a loving Father who understands perfectly all our struggles and pain. Rather than leaving us to navigate this world alone, he offers us his hand and his support every step of the way. Jesus came to this world and underwent all its evils because he wanted to save us and be near us, and the same holds true today.

We can find comfort and encouragement in the fact that his desire for us is a deep and active relationship. His promise is that we call on him in our troubles. We don't need to disguise our difficulties from him. Rather than hide or pretend that everything is okay, invite him into your hurting heart. He understands.

*Jesus, thank you for setting an example that I can follow. The life you led on earth was wrought with difficulties and heartaches, yet you did not stumble at any point. You were tempted and did not sin. Help me, Lord Jesus, to live with your strength, covered by your grace and love.*

# GOD LISTENS

*The Lord is close to the brokenhearted;*
*he rescues those whose spirits are crushed.*
PSALM 34:17 NLT

God does not grow weary or sleep; he doesn't leave or get bored. He hears our prayers and our cries for help and gives us exactly what we need. It can sometimes feel like God isn't listening, like we are speaking to an empty room. God is our omniscient and loving Father, and he knows the right time for everything. We may think if he doesn't do exactly what we're asking, when we ask for it, everything is going to go wrong. But God is fully aware of our situations. He knows the outcome of every circumstance, and he is working on our behalf to nurture us and to bring glory to himself.

The Lord is not passive; he cares deeply for his children and our well-being. He is watching out for us and will provide us with answers to our prayers. They might not be the ones we're asking for, but they will be perfect. We must have faith that he will rescue and protect our souls, wherever we are.

*God, thank you for listening. Thank you for caring about my fears and addressing them. Help me to trust that you will answer my prayers in the best way possible. I know you love me and that you want the best for me. May I trust you to meet my needs in your wonderful way.*

# STAY CONNECTED

*Rejoice with those who rejoice,*
*weep with those who weep.*
ROMANS 12:15 NRSV

In the garden of Gethsemane, on the night Jesus would be arrested and later brutally executed, he had one simple request of his friends: that they stay awake and be with him. He fully understood the horror that he was about to endure, and in this vulnerable night of grief and surrender, Jesus wanted his friends to be there with him.

Do we weep with those who are hurting, grieving loss, or frightened by the future? Sitting in another person's sorrow is uncomfortable, but it is a necessary piece of the gospel. As the body of Christ, in gratefulness of what he went through for us, we share in each other's joy and pain alike. Burdens are lighter when they are shared. Joy is greater amongst friends. Pain is more bearable with someone else.

*Teach me, dearest Savior, to sit in sorrow. I am willing to weep with those who weep and carry others' burdens with them. Please, help me not to focus on what is convenient or comfortable for me, but to actively and obediently be your hands and feet here on the earth.*

# LIMITLESS

*"Whatever you ask in prayer, believing,*
*you will receive it all."*
MATTHEW 21:22 NASB

This promise was Jesus' way of telling his disciples that if they had faith in God's power, without doubting it, they would no longer be limited to their own abilities. God's power is limitless, and there is nothing we can ask of him that he is unable to do. This doesn't always mean that he will give us what we want. It does mean that if we put all our trust in him, he will take care of us, and our needs will be met.

As we learn God's heart, our desires will align more closely with his own, and the things we ask for will cease to resemble a spoiled child's request. We will act more as stewards serving their leader and tending to their property. This world is God's, and everything in it. He wants the best for us and his kingdom.

*Lord, help me to remember that your power is far above anything I am. I don't have to be afraid of what the world can do to me, because you reign over it and will give me everything I need. Teach me to put all my trust in you, leaving my doubts behind.*

# SECURITY

*Whoever walks in integrity walks securely,*
*but he who makes his ways crooked will be found out.*
PROVERBS 10:9 ESV

There is no hope in wrongdoing. When we abandon our morals, even in the smallest way, we are haunted by the idea of being "found out." It is frightening because we have no security in wrongdoing. The writer of this proverb does not need to appeal to our emotion to convince us to avoid wrongdoing when the fact speaks for itself.

God does not want us to be afraid if we are walking in integrity. Without condition, he promises us that we will walk securely when we walk with a clear conscience. There is no punishment awaiting those who walk in faith, for Christ has paid for not just our past sins, but also for every misstep we will take. We have no reason to fear, knowing that God grants security to those who seek integrity.

*I am secure, Lord Jesus, in the path you have set before me. I have no reason to be afraid, no reason to doubt. Remind me today of the insecurity of crooked ways and the strong hand you will lead me with in life.*

# RUN THE RACE

*I know that I have not yet reached that goal,*
*but there is one thing I always do.*
*Forgetting the past and straining toward what is ahead.*
PHILIPPIANS 3:13 NCV

Paul confessed that he did not completely understood the full power of Christ's love and resurrection, but he stayed constant in his journey of following Jesus. He compared his faith walk to a race: training, straining, and pushing toward the prize at the end. We are at times left exhausted, but the end goal is worth it all. Each of us is on a journey of sanctification, and there is grace for us. Just like a real race, looking back will distract us and slow us down, so we must not dwell on past mistakes. Our focus should be forward on what God is doing in our lives, and where he is leading us.

Paul attested to knowing this well. Many Christians were persecuted and executed with Paul's (or Saul's) approval, yet he refused to let that hold him back from his newfound faith and his mission to share the good news of the gospel. God's grace is far greater than our mistakes, and our call is to leave the past behind while straining for what is ahead.

*It is not enough for me, God, that you be one of my goals in life. I want the goal of my entire life to be to serve you. You are my reward, my reason for racing, and the prize I cling to. Thank you for forgiving my past mistakes and giving me a future.*

# PRAISE THE LORD

*Praise the Lord in song, for He has done glorious things;*
*Let this be known throughout the earth.*

ISAIAH 12:5 NASB

Isn't the Lord marvelous? Hasn't he done excellent things for us and throughout the world? He is so much more deserving than the praise we can offer him, and yet it is still what he asks for. Our hearts were made to love and worship him. We find fullness when we are in touch with him and grateful for his grace.

As part of the body of believers scattered across the planet, we have the opportunity at any time and in any place to join in the global worship being offered up to him. His name is known throughout all the earth, and his greatness will always be proclaimed. Let's add our voices to the praise and offer our thankfulness to our beloved and majestic Savior.

*You are the Maker of the forests and mountains, the sunrises and snowfalls. Father, I gratefully and lovingly praise your name! Thank you for all the excellent things you have done for me.*

# ONE THING

*The Lord answered her, "Martha, my beloved Martha. Why are you upset and troubled, pulled away by all these many distractions? Are they really that important? Mary has discovered the one thing most important by choosing to sit at my feet. She is undistracted, and I won't take this privilege from her."*

LUKE 10:41-42 TPT

We are all guilty of occasionally allowing the endless cares and responsibilities of this world distract us from our true purpose. We were made to spend time with our Maker, loving him and worshiping him. Small or big, any issue that pulls us away from our only source of strength and peace must be put into check, else we jeopardize trading our souls for temporary accomplishments. Our ultimate goal is Christ, and all else follows after.

To keep from becoming ensnared in the myriad of pressing matters that beat against us daily and vie for every waking moment, it is essential that we prioritize our relationship with our Lord first. Sit with him daily. Soak in his words and his love. Let all be done out of gratitude for him, and desire him above all else. He is your "one thing" needed.

*Remind me daily, oh God, to sit at your feet and rest. The pressure of this life can be so heavy, but you restore the strength of the faithful. You lighten the load of your children, and you shoulder their burdens. Please, keep me from getting distracted as I look to you for love and purpose.*

# INDESTRUCTIBLE SOULS

*We can confidently say,*
*"The LORD is my helper;*
*I will not fear;*
*what can man do to me?"*
HEBREWS 13:6 ESV

As Christians, we have been released from the fear of death. Nothing can destroy our relationship with Jesus Christ, not even the taking of our lives. People can mock us, insult us, even harm us, but they cannot take away our salvation. Although it can be hard to stand unwaveringly through persecution, we are empowered by the knowledge that regardless of what happens to our bodies and minds, our souls are safe in the hands of our almighty God, who sent his only Son to die for us.

When we are afraid, we can remember that the Holy Spirit walks with us, and we do not need to fear harm. God will preserve our lives as long as he has work for us to do on earth, and when we have completed our mission, he will take us home to be with him.

*Father, I am bold and courageous because of the knowledge you have given me. I know that you are more powerful than anything and anyone on earth. Give me the opportunity to show others how amazing it is to live in that kind of freedom, so your kingdom can continue to grow.*

# RISE

*The godly may trip seven times, but they will get up again.*
*But one disaster is enough to overthrow the wicked.*
PROVERBS 24:16 NLT

God's strength means that even when ours should fail, his will not. We are, by human nature, weak. Though we fall time and time again, it is not because of moral weakness; even "the righteous falls seven times." But righteousness will assure that every time we fall, we will stand again. Our natural weakness will be joined by supernatural resilience.

Since we are all bound to fail, fall, and probably to do so beyond recovery at least once, who do we have to trust in? Who do we have to raise us up when we are shattered? Sin is enjoyable in times of comfort, but brokenness is the wakeup call to show us how it gives us no security. God causes the righteous to rise again seven times, but he has no relationship with the wicked. The person who does not believe in God has no hope that God will help them in times of trouble; they will be alone in their brokenness.

*Dear Lord, you are great, and you are the only one worthy of my trust. Right now, I am weak and imperfect, but you have promised to exalt me every time I fall. Thank you, Lord, for being my refuge and helper.*

# DO UNTO OTHERS

*"Do not judge, and you will not be judged;*
*do not condemn, and you will not be condemned.*
*Forgive, and you will be forgiven."*
LUKE 6:37 NRSV

Often this verse is gravely misinterpreted to mean we should not confront sin or distinguish between the good and evil actions of others. However, there is a definite Scriptural difference between discernment and condemnation. God is the judge of all, and he rules with a just and loving hand. We are his messengers, here to share the news of how wonderful and powerful he is.

Through the teaching of the Bible and the leading of the Holy Spirit, we can lovingly approach others about their sin with patience and humility. Still, our first endeavor should be to recognize and address the sin in our own lives while being quick to forgive others. Only God can judge, because only he knows our hearts.

*When confrontation is needed, dear Lord, please flood my heart with love and patience. I want to embrace others with the same care and compassion you have shown me. I also ask that you help me address the sin in my own life. I praise you, God, for your forgiveness!*

# PRACTICAL LOVE

*Whoever does not care for his own relatives, especially his own family members, has turned against the faith and is worse than someone who does not believe in God.*

1 TIMOTHY 5:8 NCV

If we love someone, are we willing to suffer for them? If not, our love is only infatuation and not the servant-like love of Christ. God wants us to love our family and the church with the same love he loved us. He wants us to love them by providing for them, caring for them, and placing them before ourselves. This is true love.

Paul goes so far as to say that any Christian who does not provide for their household "has denied the faith and is worse than an unbeliever" (NLT). He is trying to separate the true children of God from those who affect a sense of religion but do not seek after virtue. Paul wants Christians to be known for their hard work, their diligence, their love for family, and their true righteousness, and this is what it means to provide for our family.

*Lord, I pray today that my God-given responsibility to provide for my family would not burden me, but rather encourage and give me a reason to work with all energy. May I strive to bear your love in caring for others above myself.*

# HIS PRESENCE

*"My presence will go with you,
and I will give you rest."*
EXODUS 33:14 ESV

On the mornings when we are exhausted, the nights when loneliness creeps in, or when anxiety gets the better of us, we can find rest in remembering that we are never truly alone. One of the devil's ploys is to overwhelm us with cares of this world and other burdens which are no longer ours to carry.

Instead of allowing him to feed us lies, let us fill our minds with the truth of God's Word. His presence will go with us wherever we go. He will give us rest and refresh us whenever we feel weary. We do not need to play the devil's game. Remember the promises of our Lord and find peace in the most difficult of days.

*Thank you for your sweet rest and the peace that comes from knowing you. I know that I am never alone because your Spirit goes with me. Fear and loneliness no longer have a place in my life.*

# ABIDE

*Let what you heard from the beginning abide in you.*
*If what you heard from the beginning abides in you,*
*then you will abide in the Son and in the Father.*
1 JOHN 2:24 NRSV

Habits take work. It's not easy to wake up early, eat healthy, or pray every day. Good habits require effort to start and maintain them. Missing a day in our habits isn't always catastrophic, but once we've missed a day, it gets easier to justify missing just one more day, and another, until we find ourselves back at the beginning.

If we want God's truth to remain in our hearts, we must cultivate the habits of reading his Word and praying faithfully, as well as wanting to know him better. We do not find ourselves at the feet of grace by accident, but by God's great mercy. God has offered his gift of forgiveness to anyone who will take it. If we accept this gift, and abide in God's word, we will also abide in him. This means that though we currently live in a broken world, our life is in Jesus Christ, and that is a treasure that cannot be taken away.

*Lord, I ask you to ready my heart and prepare it to hear your Word and grow deep roots. I do not want your truth to be a fleeting moment in my life. I want it to remain and flourish and change me forever. Thank you for giving me your eternal gift of mercy.*

# TRUE HUMILITY

*When you do things, do not let selfishness or pride be your guide.*
*Instead, be humble and give more honor to others than to yourselves.*
PHILIPPIANS 2:3 NCV

Humility does not conceal the truth; it reveals it. If we choose to consider ourselves worth less than everyone else, then we are lying about the equal worth of all people. That is why Paul says, "count others more significant than yourselves" (ESV). It is irrelevant who is better or worse. What really matters is how significant people are to us. If we are to live as Christians, then we must focus on the success of others, whom God has called us to consider significant.

Acts of selfishness or conceit occur when people choose to ignore God's providence for them. We are never instructed to neglect our own well-being, but prioritizing success is an effective way of de-prioritizing God and other believers. Paul admonishes us to do nothing out of selfish ambition. Ambition aims at success, but true success only results from following God.

*Lord, remind me of the futility of my ambitions.*
*Give me the eyes to see others as important and worth*
*my investment. Only you can grant me prosperity and*
*achievement, so I entrust my goals to you. My efforts are*
*not enough.*

# INCREASE OUR FAITH

*The apostles said to the Lord, "Increase our faith."*
LUKE 17:5 NLT

When we read that the people who were closest to Jesus asked him to increase their faith, it should help us to see that it's okay to ask for help. The apostles witnessed Jesus doing miracles with their own eyes, and they still weren't totally convinced. We do not have to be afraid of our doubts. We can confront them, ask God to help us see clearly, and put our faith in him.

Being honest about our lack of faith is not a sin but trying to hide it or ignore it can lead to worse consequences. When we stuff down our doubts, they don't go away. They pile up under the surface until we end up with more questions than answers, and our faith sits on a very unstable foundation. God desires us to ask him the hard questions, so that he can either answer them and give us insight, or not, but still increase our faith.

*God, I pray that you would increase my faith. I know and confess that I doubt you often, and I want to be better. Please teach me to put my trust in you.*

# BY GRACE

*Remember this: sin will not conquer you, for God already has! You are not governed by law but governed by the reign of the grace of God.*
ROMANS 6:14 TPT

Although we may stumble and mess up at times, sin does not maintain dominion over us. We have been purchased at a high price, and we do not need pay extra fees. Rather than attempt to repay what is impossible, we rejoice greatly for the grace freely given to us.

Out of gratitude and joy, let us worship and serve the Lord. We have no debt. We have no other master but the Lord God Almighty. It is not out of obligation or guilt that we proclaim his name, but because of the love that overflows within us.

*You are just and loving, Father God! Your forgiveness is forever, and your compassion is complete. Thank you for the gift of grace and for separating me from my sinful nature. I want to spend my life loving you.*

# THE LORD SEES ME

*All my longings lie open before you, Lord;*
*my sighing is not hidden from you.*
PSALM 38:9 NIV

Unlike empty promises in our pasts or people who disappointed us, God Almighty hears us and responds every single time we cry out to him. Perhaps his responses are not what we expected or hoped for, but they are always loving and perfect. When we are at our most vulnerable and broken, he offers relief and comfort. He does not always remove us from our trials, but he takes our hands and guides us through them.

So much can be learned through suffering and through learning to lean on God, and he knows the best path for each of us. His ways are far superior to our ways, and so he teaches us how to walk. He holds us when we cry. He collects our tears and remembers every one of our hurts. Nothing escapes his notice, and he cares deeply and intimately for each and every one of us.

*Take my burdens, dear Father, and lead me where I should go. When life is too hard, help me walk. You always go with me, and you never leave me to struggle alone. Show me your purposes in my struggles, and lead me to your victory, I pray.*

# REMEMBER TO SHARE

*Do not forget to do good and to share,*
*for with such sacrifices God is well pleased.*

HEBREWS 13:16 NKJV

Instead of falling into a rhythm or a zone and going through life unaware of the needs around us, we need to stay vigilant to what the Holy Spirit is doing. There may be someone who needs a friend, some help, or some financial aid. We do not have the capacity to help everyone who needs it, but if we are being led by the Holy Spirit and listening to what he is telling us, we will know how to give our time, money, and emotions in the greatest way possible; a way only God can see and figure out.

Whatever way we are directed, it is important that we remember to share. All that we have has been given to us by God. Even if we earned it ourselves, he supplied us with the abilities and opportunities. God is pleased when we make sacrifices for others and share what we have, not just skim off the top but to open our very lives up to others.

*Father, you shared your love, your life, and your whole world with me. You have given me everything I need. Help me to see those around me who I can likewise share with and bless.*

# GIVEN

*"Everything that the Father gives Me will come to Me, and the one who comes to Me I certainly will not cast out."*
JOHN 6:37 NASB

Christ loves unequivocal statements. He speaks of "all" and "whoever," not "most" or "some." If the Father plans to entrust our souls to his Son, to the Son we will go. There is no other possibility, no matter how much we fight to resist God's plan. Once he sets his eyes on us, his will is absolute. His will is absolute each and every time he brings someone to his Son.

In the same way, the Son is absolute in never turning away anyone who comes to him. If the Father brings us to our knees, the Son will surely redeem us. He will not hold our sins against us, nor pardon us partially, but will fully and completely forgive us. Christ has promised not to cast out whoever comes to him, so why do we hesitate?

*Oh Jesus, how graciously you offer forgiveness. You exclude none; you cast out none. You hold me faithfully and promise to never let me go. Today, teach me to lean on that promise.*

# BETTER TOGETHER

*Let us aim for harmony in the church*
*and try to build each other up.*
ROMANS 14:19 NLT

What do we cling to? Our liberties or our brothers and sisters? Do we care more about our freedom or about our family in the faith? How far are we willing to go to fight for others and to maintain peace within the body of Christ? Although it is difficult to journey with others, we are undoubtedly better together. And although the church is imperfect, she is the chosen bride of Christ. If he refuses to give up on her, then we ought not to, either.

Our aim is to not only be part of the global church of believers, but to humble ourselves and work for harmony amongst its members. Avoidance is not the advice Paul gives; he tells us that we are to build each other up. By submitting to God, setting aside our "rights," and encouraging others with self-control and selflessness, the church of God will truly be better together.

*Lord, teach me to care more about others than my own allotted liberties. Help me to act with care and moderation toward others, and with intentionality and patience for those who are weak in the faith. May I not impute judgment on my brothers and sisters, instead aiming for harmony as much as I can.*

# JUNE

Be kind and compassionate to one
another, forgiving each other,
just as in Christ God forgave you.

EPHESIANS 4:32 NIV

# KEEP THEM CLOSE

*Let not steadfast love and faithfulness forsake you;*
*bind them around your neck;*
*write them on the tablet of your heart.*
PROVERBS 3:3 ESV

Our faithful and steadfast Lord demonstrates his love for us so that we have a perfect example to learn from and follow. Love is the trademark of a follower of God because love is who he is. If we claim to be Christians, love should define us. Love is not a fleeting feeling or a bartering chip. Love is neither fair nor easy. Today's proverb instructs us to wrap love and faithfulness around our necks and write them on our hearts because love is very, very difficult.

Love considers others, even when they are inconsiderate. Love serves others even when we don't want to. Love is steadfast through the hard times and unshaken when everything around us is easily disrupted and dismantled. Love is not a seeker of instant gratification or temporary pleasure. To choose God is to choose love, and to choose a life of love often entails the harder path. But it is by far the grander, eternal, more worthwhile option. We were made for love.

*Even when I don't feel loving, I pray that you help me to love like you, Lord Jesus. I don't want to become dissuaded by the responses of others or the flesh's desire for the easier path. I will cling to you and follow your example, binding love and faithfulness around my neck and writing them on my heart.*

# THE LORD'S DAY

*This is the day the LORD has made;*
*We will rejoice and be glad in it.*
PSALM 118:24 NKJV

Every day, we have the opportunity to recognize the gift we have been given and rejoice. The Lord's creations are good. Each day was crafted by him for us to be glad in. Rather than allow the world to impress upon us its hopelessness, let's make an impression on the world: one of hope, gladness, and rejoicing! We can live differently, full of life and love.

Instead of treating each day like a task, we can embrace each one like the blessing that it is. All around us are examples of his handiwork and his creativity. His love is evident everywhere if we simply open our eyes and our hearts to recognize it.

*How can I use today for your glory, God? What is your intention for the next twenty-four hours? What blessings have you poured into today? Please open my eyes to see your beauty and recognize what you are doing. I praise you for what you have created and rejoice in knowing you today.*

# LOVE YOUR NEIGHBOR

*"Love the LORD your God with all your heart,*
*all your soul, all your strength, and all your mind."*
*Also, "Love your neighbor as you love yourself."*
LUKE 10:27 NCV

Although we are undeserving of his love, our heavenly Father offered us his hand, his grace, and his salvation. In the same way, we are expected to love our neighbors with the care and intentionality with which we love ourselves. Whether or not we deem them worthy of love is not a factor. Christ loved us when we were wholly unworthy.

The sort of love we are called to extend is more than simply distant tolerance. It's active and deliberate. If we want to use all our hearts, souls, strength, and minds to love the Lord, then the best way to show him this love is by loving his children. With all we have and with we are, let's love our neighbors because of our love for God.

*Who would you like me to show love to today, Lord Jesus? How can I show my love and loyalty for you in the way I treat others? Please give me opportunities to love others like I love myself.*

# NUMBERED DAYS

*Teach us to number our days,*
*that we may gain a heart of wisdom.*
PSALM 90:12 NIV

Life can seem incredibly long, especially on the days we have nothing going on or when we're waiting for something. But life is fleeting. Before we know it, we're ten years older and wondering what we have to show for it. In today's psalm, Moses asked God to show his people just how important every day was. Too often we squander our time by seeking our own pleasure instead of toiling for the sake of God's kingdom.

Wisdom is gained by knowing that our time here on earth is finite. We can either waste that time or do something for the good of mankind. Today is precious and will only come one time. Are we going to treasure it and use it to bring light into the world, or let it pass us by?

*God, remind me how important each day is. I waste so much time complaining and seeking to satisfy my earthly desires; I forget that each day is an opportunity to bring you glory. Please open my eyes to your plan for the time I have left on earth.*

# A LITTLE WHILE

*After you suffer for a short time, God, who gives all grace,*
*will make everything right. He will make you strong and support you*
*and keep you from falling. He called you to share in his glory in Christ,*
*a glory that will continue forever.*

1 PETER 5:10 NCV

Peter tells us it is only going to be a little while. Suffering turns our minutes into hours as we pray for change, for release. To believe Peter's words and view our suffering as only lasting a short time is an act of faith in itself. We cannot do this without looking to the glory in Christ, which we were called to by the God of all grace. It is his grace alone which has sustained us thus far, and it will end our suffering's "little while."

Peter knows that the afflicted need something to hope for, so he pours out the promises of God's support, strength, and renewal. The Creator of the universe has deemed the things you've lost worthy of being restored, and the faith you've displayed worthy of being established.

*God of all grace, the little while of my suffering is but a footnote to your glory. Build me up with the thought that Christ is fighting my battle and the victory is forever yours.*

# STAND TOGETHER

*If another believer is overcome by some sin, you who are godly should gently and humbly help that person back onto the right path. And be careful not to fall into the same temptation yourself.*

GALATIANS 6:1 NLT

A life without God will inevitably lead to sin and heartbreak. One who is committed to God, however, will discover a dauntless hope and peace in even the darkest of times. The Lord did not intend for us to battle alone. In everything, he promises to be with us. He also created us to stand together with others so that our chances of stumbling or being overcome by sin greatly decrease.

When we recognize that a brother or sister is overcome with sin, we should go to them in love to see how we may help them. James 5:19-20 says, "If one of you should wander from the truth and someone should bring that person back, remember this: Whoever turns a sinner from the error of their way will save them from death and cover over a multitude of sins" (NIV). When we approach someone else, it should be with grace and humility. We ourselves are only set free from sin by the power of the Lord and the forgiveness he offered us.

*Lord God, instead of using your grace as an excuse to sin, teach me to use it for the sake of others, that they may experience the same joy and freedom you give me. Please keep me from sin, for I am human and prone to wander. I need your help, especially when I am helping others.*

# FAITHFUL AND JUST

*If we confess our sins, he who is faithful and just*
*will forgive us our sins and cleanse us from all unrighteousness.*
1 JOHN 1:9 NRSV

Our Lord is both faithful and just. His faithfulness to us, his children, is complete—even to the point where he gave his own life to save us. He is just, so he does not expect nor accept payment for a debt which has already been paid in full.

There is no way for us to issue payment for our sins, any more than someone could return to a store and repay for a gift that had already been bought for them. We are called to confess our sins to him, accept his forgiveness for our own unrighteousness, and live as those who were previously prisoners to sin and now are free.

*The awareness of my sin is crushing, oh Lord, but the recognition of your saving grace is so much more profound! It moves me to laughter and tears. It changes my heart and the way I live my life. You truly are faithful and just!*

# RELATIONSHIPS

*I bow my knees before the Father,*
*from whom every family in heaven and on earth is named.*
EPHESIANS 3:14-15 ESV

The Lord created each of us to have a personal and unique relationship with him. He also made us for relationships here on earth. The bonds we have with our family and friends can offer us strength, accountability, love, safety, and more. God teaches us about his love through the Bible and prayer, but also through our interactions with others.

Throughout the Scriptures, God points us toward community and opening our lives to others. Although this will be difficult at times, we benefit so much from the wisdom and strength of others. Like a tapestry or a bouquet, our Father knew that a family of believers would fare better than a collection of individuals.

*Thank you, God, for my family and friends. Thank you for the people who have walked alongside me and helped me when I was down. Thank you for each and every one of my relationships, but most of all for the one I share with you.*

# COMFORT

*"Blessed are those who mourn,*
*for they shall be comforted."*
MATTHEW 5:4 NASB

People sometimes mourn over their own sin, the sins of others, or the depravity of this world we live in. Regardless of the reason, Christ came to overturn the plans of the enemy and to end sin. While his patience with those who are still lost gives grace for sin, we have the assurance that this fixed time is limited. The day is coming when sin and all its effects will be no more. Death does not have dominion over those who have committed their lives to Jesus Christ. He will have the final word.

Although we mourn now, or act as helpless witnesses to the mourning of others, his blessings are endless and promised. Pain is temporary, but God's comfort is eternal.

*When someone else is grieving, Father, please show me how to comfort and encourage them. When I am grieving, I pray for your comfort and encouragement to keep going and keep trusting.*

# MERCY

*You must show mercy to others, or God will not show mercy to you when he judges you. But the person who shows mercy can stand without fear at the judgment.*

JAMES 2:13 NCV

We must make allowance for mercy. In our lives, there is often no empty time slots in our calendars, no purchase outside our planned budget, and no room for error. But God commands us to live in mercy, not legality. He wants us to trust him with our time, to commit our resources to him, and to be merciful to the ones who ask it of us.

There are other ways besides broken schedules that people demand our mercy, but fundamentally they are all the same. We have a plan, or an expectation for how things should go, and others are careless or unaware and jeopardize it. But has God experienced anything different? He had a divine plan for the entire universe, and humankind messed it up. May we show mercy, as he did.

*Dear Lord, remind me that my mercy will be repaid. When I come to your judgment seat, you will not be without mercy to those who have shown mercy. Let your forgiveness continually inspire me to let my mercy triumph over my judgment.*

# TRUE PROMISES

*"I will heal them and reveal
to them abundance of prosperity and security."*
JEREMIAH 33:6 ESV

Through the prophet Jeremiah, the Lord promised the people of Judah healing, prosperity, and security. As he did then, so he continues today, offering the best of his gifts to hurting and helpless people. Even though the sins of the people of Judah often led Jeremiah to tears, the Lord never gave up on them. His compassion and grace were incredibly displayed through the multitude of opportunities he gave the people to turn to him.

We cannot accidentally miss the Lord, for he is far greater than our worst mistakes. When we are not listening, he continues to knock. He offers us healing, prosperity in the things which truly matter, and security from the worst of the devil's schemes. He is true to his promises and to his loving nature. We are the chosen recipients of an unfathomably generous and patient God.

*How can I begin to thank you for all you have given me in this life, dear Father, and for all you have in store for me in the next? The cares and disappointments of this life cannot compare to the blessings you shower on me and the promise of an eternal future with you.*

# SEEK FIRST THE KINGDOM

*"Seek first His kingdom and His righteousness,*
*and all these things will be provided to you."*
MATTHEW 6:33 NASB

As we walk through our day-to-day demands and distractions, it is not easy to keep our hearts fixed on the coming kingdom. Immediate needs and pressures around us fight for the best of our time and thoughts. Of course, we were placed in this world with all its errands, and the Lord expects us to be responsible. But what are our priorities? What is our motivation? Do we live simply to live, or are we living for God, and for what's to come?

Are our minds kingdom-focused, working daily on the conditions of our hearts and the love and care of others? Do we trust the Lord with our family, finances, health, work, and so on? Our first priority every day ought to be to seek his kingdom and his righteousness by maintaining an eternal-minded approach to living. He will take care of us and everything else will be added to us. We live here on earth, but our true home is his coming kingdom.

*Oh God, as I go about my day, open my eyes to see how even the mundane demands of this world can be undertaken in a way that brings you worship. I will seek you first, keeping in mind that your kingdom and righteousness is far superior to and more lasting than anything I've known here on earth.*

# YOUR CONFIDENCE

*The LORD will be your confidence,*
*And will keep your foot from being caught.*
PROVERBS 3:26 NASB

Far greater than any source on earth, our confidence comes from the Lord. We live differently than the rest of the world because our hope is eternal and assured. When others trust in their own strength, which can only carry them for a while, we trust in God and are therefore unshakeable.

Everyone else will eventually disappoint us, and our own power has a breaking point that will one day be realized. Even the systems of this world will inevitably fail. Only God in his omnipotence will remain infallible and complete. His kingdom is forever, and our home will be with him. He promises to help us in our weakness, and we can put our entire confidence in that.

*It amazes me, dear Lord, that the all-knowing King of the universe cares to keep me safe from the snares I would inevitably walk into on my own. I put my confidence in you because I know that you will never let me go.*

# NO FEAR

*When I am afraid,*
*I will put my trust in you.*
PSALM 56:3 NLT

Where do people usually look when they are afraid or uncomfortable? To their phone maybe, or to a friend, perhaps looking for something to distract or make them feel better. When we are afraid, we have an almighty God to trust. Our fears in this world have no grounds when confronted with the power and majesty of the Lord.

Fear is one of Satan's tools. He wants to distract us from God and make us forget who we are and the power that lives inside of us. When we experience fear, the last thing we should do is run from it. There is nothing in this world that can stand against God and win. We can face the things we are afraid of with confidence because the Holy Spirit lives in us and fights on our behalf. The Bible says that nothing in this world can separate us from the love of God. Even when threatened with death, we do not have to be afraid. God himself walks with us and comforts us.

*God, when I am tempted to fear, please grant me the strength to stand up against it in your name. Please, forgive me when I give in to the anxieties of this life. Use those moments to show me your steadfast love and faithfulness.*

# GROWING IN PRAISE

*Grow in the grace and knowledge of our Lord and Savior Jesus Christ.*
*To him be glory both now and forever! Amen.*
2 PETER 3:18 NIV

Christ wants us to have a full measure of "grace and knowledge." He wants us to be filled with renewal, enlightened by the true knowledge that only God can give. Some days, it's hard to see that God's purpose is for us to thrive.

Somehow, amidst pain or our daily routine, we are being taught how to thrive. Christ is refining us, carving away our imperfections and replacing them with grace and knowledge so that we may honestly say, "to him be the glory both now and forever!" For Peter to say, "grow in...our Lord and Savior Jesus Christ," is one of the highest blessings we can receive. No other path in life is more meaningful or rewarding.

*According to your will, God, help me to grow in you. May I grow in grace, that my faith would be deeper, and in knowledge, that I might understand the incalculable depths of your compassion. All glory to you, Lord God, forever and ever.*

# WHOLESOME THOUGHTS

*Think about the things that are good and worthy of praise.*
*Think about the things that are true and honorable*
*and right and pure and beautiful and respected.*

PHILIPPIANS 4:8 NCV

Negative news can fill our minds if we let it. We cannot ignore the problems surrounding us, but we can choose what we focus our attention on. Evil is all around us, and we can easily lose hope or become distraught when it becomes consumes our time. If we choose instead to keep our thoughts wholesome and dwell on the life-giving things of God, it gives us the clarity and conviction to deal with any problems that come our way.

God's truth disarms the enemy and equips us with everything we need for a life of godliness. Unlike the messages that the media push, and unlike the world's woeful cries, God's ways are good, true, honorable, right, pure, beautiful, respectable, and worthy of praise. Things such as these are worth our time and attention. Committing our thoughts to the Lord will keep us from getting dismayed over the condition of our world, and it will help us cut through all the hate to see the glory of God in this earth.

*God, I choose to fill my mind with the truth and beauty that you have set before me. Instead of all the noise and hate propagated by the world around me, I will commit my thoughts to you and to your ways. Thank you for all the marvelous alternatives you have given me. There is no shortage of your glory!*

# SELF-CONTROL

*A man without self-control*
*is like a city broken into and left without walls.*
PROVERBS 25:28 ESV

Society often praises the strength and violence of individuals who do or say whatever is on their minds. This brash, brazen method cares little about the fallout. The aggressive approach is often celebrated for its "don't care" attitude. Quiet strength goes undetected and underappreciated. Those who are impulsive, quick-tempered, and egotistical lack the self-control expected of someone who claims to model their life after Christ.

In the face of hunger, suffering, loss, false accusations, betrayal, and ultimately torture and crucifixion, Jesus always maintained his self-control and obedience to the Father. A lack of self-control, however bold and powerful it may seem, is really a demonstration of weakness. A truly strong person knows when to listen, when to wait, when and how to act. They do not hide behind outbursts of anger or grand displays of retaliation. Instead, they are intentional, precise, calm, and in submission to the Spirit of God.

*Lord, when I feel my blood pressure rise, or I am annoyed by someone trying to get under my skin, help me to calm down and submit to your better way. Keep me from stooping to the level of fools. Give me wisdom to walk away, to bite my tongue, and to act however is proper of a child of God.*

# SLOW TO ANGER

*Those with good sense are slow to anger,*
*and it is their glory to overlook an offense.*
PROVERBS 19:11 NRSV

In an age of easily offended people, God's Word once again stands in contrast to our selfish human tendencies. People crave vengeance rather than harmony, and in the end, it costs them dearly. We return insult for insult and seek blood for blood, quickly abandoning the example of selfless love and sacrifice our Lord and Savior displayed for us.

Rather than taking offense, wisdom produces peace. Those with good sense show it by controlling their emotions and not being hotheaded. Being quickly angered and easily set off are not characteristics conducive to a godly life. Overlooking petty offenses and being slow to anger brings glory to God and to the one who has shown that they are truly following in their Maker's footsteps.

*When someone does wrong and it eats away at me,*
*I pray that you would calm my heart and remind me of*
*the bigger picture, oh Lord. I want to be guided by you and*
*by your loving Spirit, not by my own emotions, which are*
*vulnerable to offense. Thank you for helping me grow in*
*this area.*

# ROLES

*Each of you should continue to live in whatever situation the Lord has placed you, and remain as you were when God first called you.*
1 CORINTHIANS 7:17 NLT

God created us to be intrinsically valuable and incredibly unique. We are each different, so that when we work together, we create something better than the sum of its parts. We contribute to each other's lives, bringing a fresh perspective to help one another see things differently. Our society struggles to accept that, although we are created equally, we are not all the same.

We don't need to have the same path in life as our best friends. We know that even though their lives look like so much fun, our path is different because we ourselves are different. Some people will have roller-coaster stories, full of crazy ups and downs, while others may have ski lift lives, a steady but slow climb to the top. The best way for us to journey through life is by appreciating everyone's differences while valuing our particular path.

*God, I can get distracted by admiring someone else's path in life, thinking they have it easier or better. Help me to focus on the things you've given me and the events you have planned for me. May I respect others' differences and accept the plan you have for me as an individual.*

# PATTERNED AFTER CHRIST

*I want you to pattern your lives after me,*
*just as I pattern mine after Christ.*
1 CORINTHIANS 11:1 TPT

Paul understood what it meant to be a mentor or role model. When he said, "pattern your lives after me," he did not speak from pride but from compassion. He wanted his listeners to know how to imitate Christ. In a world of nonbelievers, Paul offered his own life as a testimony. He did not offer all of his life as an example, though. By adding the phrase, "just as I pattern mine after Christ," he showed that he was an imperfect role model. Christ was the ultimate example and inspiration for Paul. The elements of Paul's life that imitated Christ's were the ones worth imitating.

Are we worth imitating? We will always have sin in our lives and in our behavior. The question is whether or not people can look at how we live and see Christ's influence. No one can spiritually imitate or be eternally inspired by a person whose life is devoid of Christ.

*Lord, help me to be a worthy imitator of you today. Let my life mirror the grace and kindness you showed in your time on earth. There will always be faults and sin in my life, but don't let them conceal the light of your glory.*

# NO CONDEMNATION

*There is now no condemnation at all
for those who are in Christ Jesus.*
ROMANS 8:1 NASB

We were drowning in our wrongdoings before the Lord pulled us out and forgave us. His grace is so complete that no condemnation can follow us. Our pasts are covered with the blood of Jesus Christ, and a second payment is not due. The devil cannot condemn us, though he tries to by constantly reminding us of our failures and attempting to coerce us into guilt. Other people cannot condemn us because they have not yet themselves found freedom, and their mindsets are slaves to sin.

No. There is truly no condemnation placed on those of us who are born again in Christ Jesus. He has spoken, and it is so. Regardless of what the devil, other people, or even our own hearts tell us, we are set free and no longer live under condemnation.

*Dearest Jesus, thank you for your sacrifice, for your forgiveness, and for your love. Whenever I am tempted to live under guilt or condemnation again, please remind me of your words; your forgiveness is complete!*

# FAITH

*"You don't have enough faith," Jesus told them. "I tell you the truth,*
*if you had faith even as small as a mustard seed, you could say to this*
*mountain, 'Move from here to there,' and it would move.*
*Nothing would be impossible."*

MATTHEW 17:20 NLT

Faith is what binds us to God's will. It gives us a sense of what God
desires and helps us believe that he can make it happen. It is not
so much us getting God to do what we want to happen, but rather
God getting us to ask for what he desires. With faith, we can ask for
the right things and believe that God is powerful enough to make
them happen.

Jesus said that if we have faith like a grain of mustard seed,
mountains will move. Many people misinterpret this phrase. They
believe that they can only move mountains if they have incredible
amounts of faith. But the measure of our accomplishments is a
measure of God's strength, working through us while we pray to be
as faithful as we can, even if our faith feels as small as a mustard seed.

*Anything is possible, Lord. Please, let my faith not be*
*limited by fear or by doubt. Embolden my heart in you and*
*make me ready to ask for what is right. I give you this day*
*and everything in it.*

# CARE FOR OTHERS

*Let each of you look out not only for his own interests,
but also for the interests of others.*

PHILIPPIANS 2:4 NKJV

When we pray, how much of it is consumed with requests for protection and blessing for ourselves? Do we take time to simply praise God for who he is and what he has done? Do we beseech him on behalf of others? When someone else has a problem, are we quick to help in their time of need? Do we care for others the same way we care for ourselves, remembering that we are all parts of the same body?

It is not God's intention that we care only for ourselves and stay at a safe distance from the mess of life and others' problems. If we love God, we will care for his people. If we are truly members of the body of Christ, we will be affected when someone else is affected.

*God, please help me get out of my head and my safe, secure life. I do not want to live in fear of getting my hands dirty or allowing others with issues into my life and heart. In a world that preaches that we ought to look after number one, I recognize that you are my number one! May my life be a living praise to you.*

# A STEADFAST GOD

*If we are faithless, he remains faithful—*
*for he cannot deny himself.*
2 TIMOTHY 2:13 ESV

God never changes. He is, he was, and he is to come. Always and forever, God is steadfast and holy. We as humans cannot achieve this kind of unwavering perfection because we are flawed. We make mistakes every day. Despite this, we do not have to despair because God is forgiving, and he loves his children more than we could imagine. No matter how many times we fail, he is there, waiting for us to ask for his help.

Sometimes, it's hard to admit when we make mistakes, because we don't want others to see our flaws. But when we do, we give ourselves the opportunity to learn and try again. God is not intimidated by our mistakes. If we think there's anything God cannot do, we are limiting our all-powerful Creator. Whether we sin a hundred times or a million times, God will always be holy.

*Father, I mess up so often, and it can get discouraging to fall so short of your perfection. Please heal my broken heart and help me to remember that your goodness doesn't change when I do. Your holiness remains when everything else passes away.*

# WHEREVER YOU GO

*"Have I not commanded you?*
*Be strong and of good courage;*
*do not be afraid, nor be dismayed,*
*for the LORD your God is with you wherever you go."*
JOSHUA 1:9 NKJV

God is almost indignant with Joshua, the leader of God's people, as he commands once again, "Be strong." He is trying to get it into Joshua's head that fear of danger is not a factor in God's plan. Neither is there reason to be dismayed or weak. In the relationship between Joshua and God, there is very little inspirational talk and plenty of practical discourse, for whether or not Joshua is afraid, it does not change the reality of God's power and faithfulness.

Similarly, we sometimes forget that believing is not a matter of wishing something to be true but knowing that it is. To believe that there is no reason to be afraid is only rational. To draw away from God's promises in disbelief is the most irrational thing we can do as human beings.

*Oh Lord, why do I lack faith? Why do I fool myself into thinking that it is wiser to doubt you than to trust your testimony? Show me, oh God, that there is no reason to be afraid. Help me to be strong in my faith and my actions, even when I'm afraid.*

# REVIVE ME

*Consider my affliction and my trouble,*
*and forgive all my sins.*
PSALM 25:18 ESV

King David was an emotional writer. The book of Psalms is full of chapters praising God, begging for help, and tearfully asking for forgiveness. David wasn't embarrassed of expressing his feelings or immoralities; he took them to God and asked for assistance.

We are always lacking in some respect or another. We get into bad situations, we make mistakes, and we end up way over our heads. But God is always there, ready to forgive and to heal us. He won't force us to accept his help. He wants us to invite him into our hearts willingly and waits for us to do so. He forgives us of all our sins when we ask with a humble heart. David learned the hard way to take his troubles to God instead of trying to hide them. We can learn a lot from David's experience.

*God, you are kind and loving beyond my comprehension. Thank you for continuing to forgive me. Help me to continue to seek you and give you my mistakes.*

# LIVING WATER

*"He who believes in Me, as the Scripture has said,*
*out of his heart will flow rivers of living water."*
JOHN 7:38 NKJV

Our lives are so much richer when we believe in the Lord Jesus Christ and trust his Word. We can make plans, earn incomes, grow a family, and devote ourselves to exercise and healthy eating, but true living comes only from God. Our hearts will never be more joyful and more alive than when we are growing in his Word and our relationship with him.

Living water. What imagery! Picture life-giving water flowing from the words, actions, even the smiles of someone who is devoted to living her life according to the Scriptures. We have been given an incredible gift, not only in the love of God, but in the mission to share this love with others. What an honor. What a life!

*Thank you for filling me with your love, Father. I will do my best to share your love with others. When people see me, I want them to recognize you. You are my life, my refreshment, my comfort, and my living water.*

# FORGIVE FREELY

*"If you forgive those who sin against you,
your heavenly Father will forgive you.
But if you refuse to forgive others,
your Father will not forgive your sins."*

MATTHEW 6:14-15 NLT

How can we expect God to freely and graciously grant us forgiveness if we are not willing to forgive others? Unforgiveness is not overlooked by God. Those people we are refusing to forgive are God's creation and beloved children as well. By refusing to forgive them, we deny their importance to God.

All of us need forgiveness and healing. Every sin separates us from God, so every sin is destructive. If we fool ourselves into believing our sin is less appalling than someone else's, we assume the role of judge and disbelieve that God has power to redeem. Their sin is between them and God. Our role—our commandment—is to forgive others because our King has forgiven us.

*Oh God, please give me the heart to forgive others. At times, I get so offended and hurt. People can be cruel when they are not living in your love. Rather than allow that to embitter me, help me to exchange hate for love and forgive them.*

# A GOD WHO CARES

*"The very hairs of your head
are all numbered."*
MATTHEW 10:30 NKJV

If the problems we face seem to portray an uncaring Creator, we can rest assured that nothing is further from the truth. He allows problems to continue for our sake and the sake of the gospel, but it is not because he doesn't care. He cares so deeply for each of us that even the number of hairs on our head are known to him. He knows every tear, fear, smile, and desire hidden in our hearts.

When we consider the wonder of creation around us, every different culture and terrain on earth, we must realize that God understands it all and is aware of every detail. That speaks of a God who cares. He is not distant or removed; he created us to enjoy and to love. The hairs on our heads are numbered, and our days are numbered, but we are definitely more than a number to him. Each of us is a beloved daughter or son who was carefully fashioned and known.

*Thank you for hearing the whispers of my heart, Father God. Thank you for catching my tears and loving my laughs. I am so loved by you, and I love you back! I know that I can entrust you with all my needs and all my secrets.*

# AUTHORITY OVER ALL

*"All authority in heaven and on earth
has been given to me."*
MATTHEW 28:18 NIV

What we do, we do not do by our own authority. Whatever we do, we do by the authority of Christ. Only he has enough authority to rightfully accomplish what needs to be done. For it is not just an authority to do earthly things, but an "authority in heaven and on earth." We can be bold, then, in how we act. We are stewards of Christ's ministry, not independent agents of change.

When we rely on our own strength or authority, we make the gospel about us instead of Christ. The gospel does not exist to glorify our abilities as Christians, because we are just created people who are unworthy of praise. God made us to glorify him, which in turn glorifies us as children of our Father in heaven. Christ has been given all authority because all glory is due to him.

*Lord Jesus Christ, all glory comes through you and is due to you. Make me into an ambassador of your glory, bringing your kingdom to those around me. Help me to see where I can act on your behalf today, because you have sufficient authority to do all things.*

# JULY

"Blessed are the gentle,
for they shall inherit the earth."

MATTHEW 5:5 NASB

# EDIFYING WORDS

*Do not let any unwholesome talk come out of your mouths,*
*but only what is helpful for building others up according to their needs,*
*that it may benefit those who listen.*

EPHESIANS 4:29 NIV

The power of our words can be greatly underestimated. We can build others up or break them down, depending on the words we choose. It is our responsibility to refuse to utter any unwholesome talk, gossip, lies, slander, and so on. As children of the King, we ought to choose words that are true, encourage others, and praise God.

Since we are the Lord's creation and made in his image, it is shameful when we act disgracefully. We represent him and are made to bring him praise. How can we worship God one moment, then turn and curse someone else who was made in his image? James warns against this destructive behavior (James 3:5-6).

*Please guard my mouth, Father God, and teach me to think before I speak. Let my words edify others and glorify you. I will not allow unwholesome talk to come from my mouth, instead keeping all of my words and thoughts captive. Please use me to encourage others.*

# ONLY TRUE GUIDE

*Every person's way is right in his own eyes,*
*But the LORD examines the hearts.*
PROVERBS 21:2 NASB

The Lord sees beyond our actions into the motivations of our hearts. The amazing thing is that he still loves us. For him, everything traces back to the condition of our hearts. Why are we doing these actions? Are we trying to win his favor somehow? Or are we so filled with gratitude for him that goodness pours out of us?

Our ways may seem right to us and to others who are watching, but what the Lord really wants is a loving and real relationship with each of us. Like any other relationship that is only based on actions and trying to impress, it won't last without a real heart connection. Instead of putting on an appearance of holiness, we should strive to follow God and fall in love with him. He is our only true guide and will never lead us astray.

*Even when my actions appear godly to others, help me evaluate myself based on my relationship with you, dear God. When it looks like I'm falling apart and I keep making mistakes, I know that it is you I answer to, and you see when I am trying my best. Thank you for your grace and for desiring a relationship with us.*

# GOD'S OWN

*They desire a better, that is, a heavenly country.*
*Therefore God is not ashamed to be called their God,*
*for He has prepared a city for them.*
HEBREWS 11:16 NKJV

Although the earth is an incredible display of God's power and creativity, it is not his final intention for us. He made us to dwell with him, and his home is where we belong. If we feel like we don't fit into the world's systems, it is because we were created for something more. God made us to walk with him, talk directly with him, live in his kingdom, and worship before him. All of this was stripped away when we were separated by sin, but one day we will return to our intended conditions again.

We desire a home that we have not yet seen because God has hidden eternity in our hearts (Ecclesiastes 3:11). He intends to satisfy this desire one day by bringing us home to him. Our perfect, almighty God does not feel any shame in identifying with us, even though we constantly fall victim to our own imperfections. He has prepared a perfect, eternal city for us to one day call home.

*Thank you, Father, for not condemning me for my flaws. You are not ashamed to call me your child. I wait eagerly to finally return home to you.*

# TRUE FREEDOM

*"Then you will know the truth,
and the truth will make you free."*
JOHN 8:32 NCV

We've all felt that sinking feeling when we give into temptation and lie. It's an ugly feeling, one of guilt, shame, and anger. Jesus says that anyone who practices sin is a slave to it. Sin rules our hearts when we accept it into our lives. The idea that we can control our sin, that we can stop at any time, is a lie. Sin commands us, not the other way around.

The only one with the power to break the bond between us and sin is Jesus Christ. Only he can free us from our spiritual slavery. He has paid that price and given us the option to choose life. Knowing this, we not only can walk away from our mistakes, but we also have power over our fear. In Jesus, we know that he has set us free forever. Sin has no control over our lives because Jesus is more powerful, and he has freed us from it.

*God, thank you for giving me a way out of sin. Thank you for redeeming me in full and making me your child. You love me so much more than I deserve, and I want to honor that by obeying your Word and turning away from my sin.*

# ALTERNATIVES

*I'm afraid that just as Eve was deceived by the serpent's clever lies,*
*your thoughts may be corrupted and you may lose your*
*single-hearted devotion and pure love for Christ.*
2 CORINTHIANS 11:3 TPT

There are many alternatives to Christ. Worldly religious leaders cloak themselves under the guise of Christianity when all they have to offer is the world, not Christ crucified. We hear false promises of peace, prosperity, fulfillment, and forgiveness through our works. All these false versions of Christ at their core are focused on people, usually us, and what we can get out of a spiritual teaching. This is not pure devotion.

The Christian cannot sit on the throne of their own heart. We have been deeply moved by Christ's work on the cross and so our greatest pleasure is to live in devotion to Christ. We should find no spiritual satisfaction in a teaching that raises us above the level of our King. No matter how promising, no matter how bright the rewards claim to be, the versions of Christianity marketed to us will never deliver. It is only through God's Word that we will find a truly satisfying Lord and Savior.

*Gracious King, Loving Redeemer, thank you for your righteous truth. You do not fade, change, or tell me only part of who you are. Your Word forever remains the map I follow to see you in clarity and righteousness. Today, please help me to separate the true message from any false teaching.*

# SEASONS

*For everything there is a season,*
*and a time for every matter under heaven.*
ECCLESIASTES 3:1 NRSV

God's truth is constant and unchanging, but seasons are not. Our lives are comprised of different seasons, and there are lessons to be learned in each of them. Our Lord is too big for us to assume that he will always follow a pattern or that we can put him in a box. It is necessary for growth and our relationship that we go to him daily to hear his voice and learn from his leading.

Throughout the Bible, God led different people down different paths. We are not each on the same journey because God has a unique relationship with every one of his children. Our lives may change in an instant for the better or worse but through it all we can be sure that God's love remains the same.

*Good Shepherd, you lead me through valleys and over mountains, through times of plenty and deprivation, into love and heartbreak, but I know that you, Lord, remain the same. In every season, I praise you for continuing to guide and care for me.*

# VICTORIOUS FAITH

*Every child of God defeats this evil world,*
*and we achieve this victory through our faith.*
1 JOHN 5:4 NLT

When the evil schemes of this world are overwhelming and intrusive, we rest in the knowledge that the victory already belongs to us. The road is not easy, but the end is written in blood. We are God's children, and this is his story of redemption and victory.

He made the road straight for us to follow. It may be narrow and full of snares, but he promises to keep our feet from stumbling (Psalm 121:3) and to be a light for the path (Psalm 119:105), guiding us forward. With him as our guide, we are guaranteed to defeat the evil in this world and achieve his victory. There is nothing on this earth powerful enough to overcome a child of God.

*Father, regardless of all my striving, it is you who has the victory. Out of your goodness, you extend your triumph with me and save me from all the traps the of the enemy. Even death is no match for you and therefore no match for me, your child. I follow you in faith and praise you for saving me.*

# JOY OF FRIENDSHIP

*Perfume and incense bring joy to the heart,
and the pleasantness of a friend
springs from their heartfelt advice.*
PROVERBS 27:9 NIV

We all know the pleasant sensation of receiving a hug from a friend who smells nice. Imagine if that friend also offered helpful and godly advice from a place of true love and concern. What a joyful experience!

The Bible paints this lovely picture to emphasize the welcoming wonder of true friendship. It is far easier to accept advice from a true friend, one we know cares for us sincerely. And how much more pleasant if they smell nice while delivering their advice? The importance of friendship and accountability cannot be overstated.

*You are my best friend, God. It is truly wonderful that you also call me friend. Soften my heart to receive your truth and accept wise advice from others. Thank you for people in my life who love me and care about what happens to me.*

# IN HIS NAME

*"If in my name you ask me for anything,
I will do it."*
JOHN 14:14 NRSV

What is in a name? In our modern world, names don't carry as much weight as they used to in ages past. Back in the days of Jesus and John, your name was also your rank and your placeholder. In many cultures, it qualified you and proved your status in society. Looking back on history, many a decree or law was carried out in the name of the king, emperor, or presiding ruler. His or her name carried authority and power, and it was law as far as the ruler's territory extended.

Even the most powerful human names can't compare to the name of Jesus. His name supersedes that of any earthly king, lord, or modern celebrity. His name commands authority to the highest degree. Waves fall still, mountains bow down, rocks sing praises, and demons flee. The name of Jesus holds power in every situation or circumstance. Strongholds are torn down, and every yoke of illness or chain of infirmity submits to him.

*Lord, I know that when I pray in your name, you are able to help me according to your will. I ask now that you help me believe you, trusting in you each and every time I lift up your name.*

# SUSTAINED

*Even lions may get weak and hungry,*
*but those who look to the Lord will have every good thing.*
PSALM 34:10 NCV

In other translations of this verse, the psalmist says that even young lions suffer hunger. Even those in the prime of life cannot provide for their most basic needs. Why should we be any different? Why would we assume that if we plan enough and if we work hard, we will secure our future?

The Bible does not support this idea. Instead, it is those who seek the Lord who will receive what they need. This is how God wants to provide for us. Not in stress, not by our own power, but by seeking him and letting him take care of our needs. We do not ignore our own well-being for God to sustain us, but we acknowledge that all our needs are provided for by God.

*Oh God of all providence, thank you for your promises. Teach me to commit my way to you and to trust that you will provide for me. May I not grow careless or ignorant of what I require and let me show faith in believing that I will lack no good thing.*

# MANY GIFTS

*There are varieties of gifts, but the same Spirit. And there are varieties of ministries, and the same Lord. There are varieties of effects, but the same God who works all things in all persons. But to each one is given the manifestation of the Spirit for the common good.*

1 CORINTHIANS 12:4-7 NASB

There are different players in a soccer team, and each one is vital to the success of the team because they have unique roles to play. In order to score goals, each team member must play their part. If members try to mimic other players instead of playing their own roles and abilities, the whole team suffers. If the goalie suddenly becomes jealous of the midfielders and abandons his post, he leaves the net open to attack. Similarly, if the strikers retreat and want to be just defenders, the team could never score a goal, and all their efforts would be for naught.

It is the same way in the kingdom of God. We have different gifts but fight for the same team. The same Spirit guides us, and the same Lord loves us. Within our different roles, we work together to fulfill the greater purpose of advancing the kingdom of God.

*Lord, thank you for the gifts you have given to me. Help me be effective in my role while I encourage others in theirs. May we together bring glory to your name!*

# WHOLESOME BEAUTY

*You are altogether beautiful, my love;*
*there is no flaw in you.*
SONG OF SOLOMON 4:7 ESV

There is a beauty that surpasses the superficial beauty many people chase. It is pure and unmatched in splendor. This sort of wholesome beauty is found in the glory of God and in those who glorify God. Picture the exquisiteness of rainbows and oceans. The same Maker who laid out forests and designed waterfalls, who considered every creature and imagined me and you, has filled his creation with his splendor. He gazes at you and declares that you are beautiful. He is pleased with his creation of you.

In the beginning, at the time of creation, everything God made he declared good and full of beauty. Sin came and distorted that beauty, and we see the flaws and the consequences of sin in ourselves and the world around us. God's glory still permeates his creation, however, and his final restoration plan is in place.

*Lord, help me recognize true beauty and not the superficial, earthly beauty that passes away. Train me to focus on what is good and wholesome, what brings you honor and glory. Thank you for every good thing I have in my life; it all comes from you.*

# THE LORD CARES

*Cast all your anxiety on him,
because he cares for you.*
1 PETER 5:7 NRSV

Worry and anxiety accompany us all. Every day, as long as we are living, we will be plagued with worldly cares and intrusions. These can cause anxiety in even the most faithful of people. What a blessed assurance it is to know that we have a loving Father who takes all our worries and anxieties away.

Anxiety and worrying depreciate us mentally and don't add any value to our lives. Praise God that he cares for our mental states! He wants to offer us permeating peace throughout every single part of our lives. We can rest in the knowledge that he cares for us and is bigger than our problems.

*Lord God, I know you care about me and want to banish my anxiety. The worries of the world often distract my mind and fill my heart. Please, help me focus on you and not my circumstances. Give me a peace that is beyond human comprehension as I surrender all my cares to you.*

# UNLIKE ANY OTHER

*"Since the beginning of the world
men have not heard nor perceived by the ear,
nor has the eye seen any God besides you,
who acts for the one who waits for him."*

ISAIAH 64:4 NKJV

In the days of the Bible, it was common for people of various nations to have multiple gods to worship. They would give them names and attribute certain powers to them, like power over the rain, the sun, or their health.

These days, our gods are a little harder to identify. They are things we want and prioritize over everything else. They can look innocent from the outside, but if we put more importance on them than spending time with God, they take his place in our hearts. Wanting to be wealthy, have a family, or travel aren't inherently bad things. However, if we're unwilling to give them up if God asks us to, or if they become a fixation in our hearts, it's time to take a step back and figure out who our gods really are.

*When things of this world become more important to me than you, God, please help me to see clearly. Rescue me from the temptation to worship other things. Bring me back to you.*

# HELP FOR AFFLICTION

*He will care for the needy and neglected*
*when they cry to him for help.*
*The humble and helpless will know his kindness,*
*for with a father's compassion he will save their souls.*
PSALM 72:12-13 TPT

No one is alienated from all help. Even if everyone turns against the poor, needy, desperate sinners of our world, Christ has promised to be their helper. He says that he will have compassion on the needy not just in words, but in actions too.

The Lord Jesus Christ is a fair god. We see people inexplicably elevated and others senselessly persecuted in the world, but Christ is contrary to this way. For those who have received nothing on earth, he promises riches in heaven. Deliverance, help, and pity flow from the Bible as a promise to all of us still on earth.

*Jesus, you are the promise of salvation to all the afflicted. You are the help I cry out for, the deliverance I fall back on. Teach me how to show your love to others, so that they may know your generosity.*

# OBEDIENCE

*I will keep on obeying your instructions*
*forever and ever.*
PSALM 119:44 NLT

Devotion to and delighting in the Lord is something the psalmist was well acquainted with. Obedience to our Lord not only honors him; it is also good for our well-being and blesses our lives richly. Only God knows what is best for us. He understands us better than we understand ourselves.

When our delight is in the Lord and in obeying his Word, we experience a deeper fulfillment than we could ever hope for on our own. He constantly renews our spirits and refreshes our minds forever and ever. As we walk with the Lord and obey his instructions, we will discover that his way truly is the best and most effective way to live.

*Thank you, dear Lord, for the love and care you lavish upon me every day. I love your instructions and your laws, for they provide a path for me to live my best possible life. You are far wiser and more loving that I am, so I will gladly obey you and give thanks for your mandates.*

# STRONG AND BOLD

*"Be strong and bold; have no fear or dread of them,*
*because it is the LORD your God who goes with you;*
*he will not fail you or forsake you."*

DEUTERONOMY 31:6 NRSV

Fear and dread are weapons of the enemy. They are used to paralyze us and make us ineffective when we are supposed to be growing in the Lord. God is clear that we should neither fear nor be dismayed, for he is the one who goes with us.

Knowing that God is with us no matter what should fill us with courage and boldness. At times, it may feel like we are trudging alone through life and that nobody understands our plight. God has assured us that he understands, and he is always there to strengthen, guide, protect, and comfort us. Our fearlessness and boldness come from our confidence that we are already victorious in Christ.

*Victorious Lord, I look to you for strength and courage and ask that you take away my fear. No matter what dangers stand in my path, I know you are stronger than my enemies and greater than my fear.*

# THE LORD'S BLESSINGS

*"The Lord bless you and keep you;*
*the Lord make his face shine on you and be gracious to you;*
*the Lord turn his face toward you and give you peace."*
NUMBERS 6:24-26 NIV

The Lord's blessings, as recorded in the book of Numbers, were actually announcements. They were declared through Aaron, the high priest of Israel, to the Israelites as a kind of invocation from the Lord upon them. They knew that the Lord was with them wherever they went, so they could go back into the fields and work and go home to their families. They could even be carried away into captivity and later released, never doubting for a moment that their Lord was with them throughout it all.

This proclamation was important because, apart from the Lord, the Israelites toiled in vain. Similarly, if our work is not for the Lord, what is its use? We also have the assurance that the Lord is with us wherever we go. The blessings of God were important to them then, and they are important to us now.

*Almighty God, thank you for the blessings you bestow so generously upon me. Thank you for keeping me close and safe, gazing on me with love, showing grace, and giving your peace.*

# NEVER FORSAKEN

*Though he may stumble, he will not fall,*
*for the LORD upholds him with his hand.*
PSALM 37:24 NIV

Here lies our reason for entrusting the future to God's hand. Every fear and anxiety about what lies ahead has its root in the ultimate fear that we will not be able to overcome it. We worry it will crush us. Yet God allays this fear with his ultimate promise that we will not be overwhelmed.

We may be swayed by broken relationships, financial insecurity, and the death of loved ones. In the midst of these times, our voices will cry out to God, questioning why he is allowing pain to seep into the marrow of our souls. A voice will respond. Though you fall, the Lord supports you with his hand.

*Gracious Lord and Savior, bring me the strength to trust in your power today. Give me the faith needed to take one tired step toward you each hour. Let the love you have shown draw out my praise.*

# SEEKING GOOD

*In all things I have shown you that by working hard in this way we must help the weak and remember the words of the Lord Jesus, how he himself said, "It is more blessed to give than to receive."*

ACTS 20:35 ESV

When we seek our own good instead of the good of others, we are not just being selfish; we are fools. The entire Bible lays out for us how radical generosity brings life and joy where greed never could. As Paul points out, "It is more blessed to give than to receive." If we have enough of a testimony to follow from just one person in Scripture, how much more do we have in its entirety?

Giving is not always the harbinger of joy, though. For some people, so much is demanded of them that giving feels like a curse that has been leveled upon them. Yet what they are doing is investing much. Just as God told Israel, "there is a reward for your work" (Jeremiah 31:16), so there is reward for them. Exhaustion and heavy burdens will give way to praise.

*Remind me what a blessing it is to give, Lord. Give me wisdom to know where my blessing will serve you and where it will not. Today, may my viewpoint change, Lord, so that I search for the good of others in my life.*

# HOLY SPIRIT

*"The Helper, the Holy Spirit, whom the Father will send in My name,*
*He will teach you all things, and remind you of all that I said to you."*
JOHN 14:26 NASB

The role of the Holy Spirit in a believer's life is critical. It underscores all the choices we make as believers. The Holy Spirit is our guide, our partner, and our comforter. When we start to drift, he helps us remain in God's will. He shows us how to operate in our lives and our ministries.

Life as a Christian would not be effective without the Holy Spirit's input and mentorship. He enables every believer to overcome the natural tendency to sin, as well as the external pressure to do wrong. He reminds us to keep our hearts attentive to God's leading and receptive to when God convicts us of our sins. He communes with us daily, and he helps us stay sensitive to the voice of God, so that we can always know what to do when life becomes confusing. He is our counselor, our light in the darkness. He is the power of God manifested in us, a powerful ally in our walk of faith.

*Holy Spirit, I ask that you continue to guide me through life and into a closer relationship with my Maker. Please, fill me with love and gratitude and take charge of my life.*

# THREE TIMES

*I begged the Lord three times
to take this problem away from me.*
2 CORINTHIANS 12:8 NCV

Sometimes we desire what is ordinarily good, but it goes against God's will for the circumstance. We naturally dislike pain because pain is bad, even if it does lead to good things. For a while, we may recognize that our daily trials are bringing us closer to God. Those of us who have chronic suffering, physical or mental, may sometimes think it is unnecessary for our spiritual journey. Surely it is only a burden. Our natural inclination is to pray to Jesus against such pain, knowing that he withholds nothing from those he loves. But the pain continues. It continues just as it did for Paul, even after he prayed against it three times.

God's thoughts are greater than our own, and he can see how trials or pain will shape us into someone better, even if it seems impossible to us. We might think God is cruel for this, but his motivation is born out of love and a desire to make us into the image of his Son.

*Lord, give me faith to endure any pain. Help me to not doubt you, even when I ask repeatedly but do not hear from you. Give me faith enough to instead trust that your plan is good.*

# SOUND ADMONITION

*My child, give me your heart,*
*and let your eyes observe my ways.*
PROVERBS 23:26 NRSV

In a healthy relationship between a mother and her child, there is active love and mentorship. Her desire is for her children to thrive, grow, and prosper in every good thing. A godly mother wants her children to succeed, so she allows them to make mistakes while remaining close by, ready if they need her. She teaches them about good and evil, and about God. She prepares them for the days of trouble and shares her wisdom with them, so that they can navigate this difficult world.

When we give our hearts to God, we are trusting him as our guiding parent. We are saying, "Father, we trust you and want to learn all that you have to teach us." Although he safeguards us, he does not keep us ignorant of the works of the evil one. Like a godly mother, he shows us how to overcome evil with good, how to rise when we fall, and how to carry our crosses. It is not ignorant bliss to which he has called us. Through mature mentoring, personal example, and sound admonition, he sanctifies and prepares us for the road ahead.

*Father God, you want me to prosper in your ways.*
*Through you, I pray for continual growth and guidance as I*
*follow your example.*

# UNDESERVED KINDNESS

*Jesus, when He came out, saw a great multitude and was moved with compassion for them, because they were like sheep not having a shepherd. So He began to teach them many things.*

MARK 6:34 NKJV

One of the things we are shown in the gospels is God's heart for his people. He did not send a standard sacrifice to redeem us; he sent his very own Son. Jesus is fully God and fully man. In his earthly life, he had a lot of the same struggles we have, so he was able to sympathize with the people of Israel. He knew what they were going through and ached for them. He knew how lost and purposeless they were without the truth in their hearts, so he gave it to them.

Jesus was not a lecturer; he was a mentor. He was involved in the lives of the people he taught. He experienced their hurt and loved them through it. It is so wonderful to see this side of Jesus in the Bible. It helps us remember how Jesus sees us and desires to comfort us.

*Thank you so much for the compassion and love that you show me daily. I don't deserve it, but you give it so freely. Please, help me to show this kind of kindness to others without expecting anything in return.*

# ENCOURAGE ONE ANOTHER

*Encourage the hearts of your fellow believers and support one another, just as you have already been doing.*

1 THESSALONIANS 5:11 TPT

The body of Christ was made to act in harmony. It is easy to debate and question our fellow children of God, but this can only be done on a foundation of encouragement. If the foundation is gone, then all our words will crumble to the ground. Arguments will become more about winning and less about learning the truth. Words of encouragement will be replaced with criticism of life practices, and unity will fracture.

God delights when his children build each other up. When they encourage each other, an act of perfect synergy occurs, and more goodness is produced in the hearts of believers than was even invested. Here is the heart of unity and the desire of God.

*Lord, please open my eyes to the needs of my brothers and sisters in Christ. Show me the best way to build up those around us, pushing them on toward you. May I be a bringer of unity today, born out of the love and mutual care of Christ's people.*

# PURELY GRACE

*By grace you have been saved through faith;*
*and this is not of yourselves, it is the gift of God;*
*not a result of works, so that no one may boast.*
EPHESIANS 2:8-9 NASB

At some point in our lives, most of us have felt that our salvation was our own doing. Somehow, we did something to merit forgiveness. We like to think that we had a part in our sin being washed away.

It is imperative for us to remember that the grace we have been given was not earned. It was freely gifted by our merciful and loving God. We cannot earn grace; we can only accept it. If we think we can take part in earning it, we make Jesus' sacrifice meaningless. Jesus died so our sins could be forgiven, because only a pure and holy sacrifice could pay for our sins. We are not pure or holy on our own, and we are therefore unable to buy our own freedom. The taking of Jesus' life was necessary to redeem us, and it isn't something we could ever take credit for.

*God, you are the only reason that I have the option to accept mercy. I know I cannot create a way out of sin for myself, so thank you for providing one. You are truly a loving father.*

# JOYFUL IN HOPE

*Be joyful because you have hope.*
*Be patient when trouble comes,*
*and pray at all times.*
ROMANS 12:12 NCV

The apostle Paul confidently wrote to the Christians in Rome because he knew from personal experience what it meant to remain joyful through hard times. As a believer in Christ Jesus who had faced persecution from people and attacks from the devil, Paul also knew the believers of that time were certain to experience similar hardships. It was vital that they understood how to cling to hope during persecution. The simple answer? Be joyful in hope.

The hope that Christ gives us produces joy, making it apparent to all that we live for a higher calling than is found in this world. We can face affliction with resilience because we know that hardships are only momentary, while God's grace remains forever.

*Lord, thank you for the hope and joy you have given me. Your joy is eternal and unyielding under pressure. When trouble comes, I shall prevail because of my hope in you. To the glory and honor of your mighty name I pray, believing and trusting in Jesus.*

# GLORY TO COME

*I consider that our present sufferings are not worth comparing with the glory that will be revealed in us.*
ROMANS 8:18 NIV

Suffering does not need to bring us to despair. As Christians, we know that our suffering is actually working good in us, teaching us things like patience and humility. Furthermore, we know that our suffering is only temporary. Glory is to come! One day, all the pain and heartache we experience in this life will be washed away. Evil will be brought to its knees and only what is of God will remain.

The joy and peace that will overtake us will be unlike anything we've ever experienced. God gives us glimmers and tastes of what is to come, but when his full glory is finally revealed and we are made whole in his presence, all our past sufferings won't compare to the rewards he has in store for those who faithfully followed him.

*Dearest Savior, when I suffer, please remind me of your intentionality in my life. Unlike those who are lost, I suffer with purpose and with hope. My heart yearns for you, and for you I endure. I know that it will all be worth it when you make everything right.*

# OVERCOMING TEMPTATION

*No temptation has overtaken you except such as is common to man; but God is faithful, who will not allow you to be tempted beyond what you are able, but with the temptation will also make the way of escape, that you may be able to bear it.*

1 CORINTHIANS 10:13 NKJV

Our salvation does not dismiss our actions. Although we have been given grace abundantly, there are still consequences for sinful choices. The Bible gives us a set of standards, not for our salvation, but to help us live our most optimal lives and bring glory to our Lord, who redeemed us from death.

Although the temptations of this life may seem stronger than we are, God is stronger still. Like a good father, he is nearby and willing to help us whenever we ask him to. There is no temptation too strong for us because God is by our side. He always provides a way for us to escape the pressure by bearing all burdens with us, no matter what they are.

*My Father, please help me to overcome temptation. At times, I feel so weak. But when I walk with you, no power of darkness or scheme of the enemy can overtake me. I will choose to walk with you daily, for I know you are my only way to escape temptation.*

# RESENTMENT

*This change of plans greatly upset Jonah,
and he became very angry.*

JONAH 4:1 NLT

Jonah had just watched the Lord forgive a very sinful people whom Jonah wanted to see punished for their sins. He had foreseen that God would be "merciful, slow to anger and abounding in steadfast love" (verse 2) to the people of Nineveh, and he did not want this to happen! It left Jonah unsatisfied, because Jonah was human. Humans are prone to resentment.

The longer we are Christians, the easier it becomes to measure our religiousness by how much we have done for God, rather than the other way around. When we see others given God's grace in the same measure or even more, it can cut deeply. How could God bless them so much and us so little, when we are the ones who have been doing the hard work? If this is our thought, then we have fallen far from understanding the heart of our Maker. Christianity is a religion of faith, not works. If we consider God's grace a payment for our faithfulness, then we have lost sight of what grace really is: bestowed upon all, freely, beautifully, wonderfully.

*Oh God, help me overcome this present resentment. Help me to forget my works and efforts and instead rely on you. It is easy to have contempt for those who are blessed richly with grace when I feel more deserving. Please, restore me to a frame of mind that knows no one is deserving. In that frame of mind, I will be able to receive your grace.*

# STAY THE COURSE

*Since we are surrounded by so great a cloud of witnesses,*
*let us also lay aside every weight, and sin which clings so closely,*
*and let us run with endurance the race that is set before us.*
HEBREWS 12:1 ESV

Life seems so much easier when you have someone along to cheer you and inspire you to keep trying. God blesses us with people in our lives because he knows they will help motivate and encourage us. Whether we are married, have close friends, or enjoy healthy relationships with our families, we never have to run the race alone. He always provides others in the body of Christ to help us push forward.

Even if we feel utterly alone, history is filled with faithful followers of Christ who, against all odds, finished their races triumphantly. The Bible records their testimonies to encourage us in our times of loneliness or self-doubt. This cloud of witnesses is cheering us on as we race to win and endure for the sake of Christ.

*Thank you for your Word, dear God. Thank you for the people you have put in my life and for those who have gone before me. Most of all, thank you for never leaving me. You cheer me on every step of the way!*

# AUGUST

"Don't worry or surrender to your fear.

For you've believed in God,

now trust and believe in me also."

JOHN 14:1 TPT

# THE WILL OF GOD

*"Father, if you are willing, remove this cup from me.*
*Nevertheless, not my will, but yours, be done."*
LUKE 22:42 ESV

At times, it is difficult to understand the will of God in our lives. Perhaps what he is leading us to does not align with what we had planned or prayed for. It can be hard to accept God's will for us when we imagined our lives going in a different direction, especially when God's path involves suffering and pain. Regardless, he is the King, the only one who can perfectly see what is best for us. Therefore, it is important that we humble our hearts and submit to his better way.

Jesus left us a perfect example of submission to God's will when he was in the garden of Gethsemane, just prior to his crucifixion. How can we begin to fathom how it felt to accept that fate on our behalf? It was so difficult and painful for him that he sweated drops of blood! Still, he said, "Not my will, but yours be done." As believers, we are invited to surrender to God's will, even when it is contrary to what we desire. Even when it hurts or even kills us, God's will is always perfect and always good. Let us remember that the grace of God is sufficient to carry us through anything.

*Jesus, I will always remember that you suffered for my sake. Help me conform to your will whenever I face suffering or challenges. Give your strength, wisdom, and boldness when I need it.*

# THE LORD HEALS

*Heal me, LORD, and I will be healed;*
*Save me and I will be saved,*
*For You are my praise.*
JEREMIAH 17:14 NASB

Confidence in the Lord is important when we pray. In today's verse, Jeremiah knows he will be healed. Sometimes when we pray, we second-guess God, his abilities, or how much he loves us. We doubt, and in doing so, we limit our anticipation of his supernatural intervention.

God is not weak. He is not disinterested. We can be sure that whatever we ask in his name, for his glory, will happen. In our humanity, it's easy to think that God is limited or in some way inhibited. This verse reminds us that God is both willing and completely capable of reaching out and fixing our situation, no matter what we are facing.

*Lord, at times I doubt your ability or willingness to save me from sickness, problems, and sin. I feel like they are too big for you, or that you are unconcerned about me. May this verse become real in my life, to the glory and honor of your name.*

# PATIENT HOPE

*If we hope for what we do not see,*
*we wait for it with patience.*
ROMANS 8:25 NRSV

Patience is not a common trait. In fact, as technology advances, it is becoming more and more rare. We are so used to instant gratification that waiting patiently is almost a forgotten concept. People grow angry if they are kept waiting and give up easily on anything that takes long-term commitment. The conclusion to our hope is not yet here. We must wait, and wait patiently. As believers in Christ Jesus, one of the characteristics that sets us apart is patience.

Many grow weary of waiting on the Lord, and they will attempt to find solutions for life elsewhere. But this impatience only leads to ruin and frustration. The Bible is filled with examples of people who attempted to force God's hand early because they didn't want to wait, and that approach never produced good results. We are to be patient in hope because God's hope does not fail us.

*Oh Lord, I ask that you help me wait for you with thanksgiving and hope. Give me patience to endure the difficult times when I am tempted to move away and seek my own path. I pray this, believing and trusting in your goodness.*

# A GREAT REWARD

*Blessed is the one who perseveres under trial because,
having stood the test, that person will receive the crown of life
that the Lord has promised to those who love him.*

JAMES 1:12 NIV

The race that has been set before us is not easy. God promises that we are going to encounter persecution and hardship in our lives. Even everyday living can feel like running in place. The hope we have is this: the trials will end, evil will be no more, and our eternity will be spent in the presence of God. The decades we spend on earth will be more than worth the pain we go through, just to hear his voice.

Are we willing to hold fast during the evils of this life in order to spend forever in perfect peace? It seems like a simple question, but it's not easy to remember when we lose our job, a car breaks down, or someone we love gets sick. We must remember in those low moments that God can and will give us the strength to stand on solid ground and outlast the storm.

*God, please hold this hope of a perfect future at the forefront of my mind. Please, give me the power to rise when I feel weak. Help me to lean upon your strength and not my own.*

# DELIGHT

*Take delight in the Lord,*
*and he will give you the desires of your heart.*
PSALM 37:4 NRSV

When we desire what is right, God is pleased to bless us with it. Although he may withhold good things from us for a season, there is one thing that God never gives sparingly—himself. All that is a part of his righteous character will never be withheld from us. This is the will of God, as he is cultivating our desire for what is good and our disdain for what is not.

The psalmist commands, "Take delight in the Lord." God is just, loving, and abounding in majesty. In trying to do the will of the Lord, it can be difficult to slow down and see God's goodness. Yet spending time with God is his will for us. Through this we learn to delight in him, and by delighting in him, the rest of our lives will begin to make sense.

*Oh Lord, why do I allow small priorities to triumph over my delight in you? Only you, Lord, are truly delightful. There is no other who brings me joy as you do. Your goodness is an everlasting testimony to your glory, and for it I will glorify you.*

# LOVE YOUR ENEMIES

*"To you who are willing to listen,*
*I say, love your enemies!*
*Do good to those who hate you.*
*Bless those who curse you.*
*Pray for those who hurt you."*

LUKE 6:27-28 NLT

The command "love your enemies" is thrown around so much that it has become a commonly used and abused statement. When we think about the implications of what this looks like lived out, who else apart from Christ would be bold enough to teach such doctrine?

Imagine being a Jew during Biblical times. A new rabbi instructs you to love the Roman persecutor who has forcefully taken your land, overtaxed your family, and disrespected and mocked your faith as well as your way of life. Yet that was Jesus telling his followers to love their enemies. Some of his listeners may have thought he was mentally unsound. Perhaps others were offended by such a notion. The way of the cross is radically different from human wisdom. Jesus had a heavenly mentality, not an earthly one, and those who trusted him could, too.

*Father God, loving my enemies does not feel natural, and I don't always feel loving. Yet you called me to be more like you, to take up my own cross, and to follow you. Please, fill me with your love.*

# SPIRIT OF POWER

*God has not given us a spirit of fear,*
*but of power and of love and of a sound mind.*
2 TIMOTHY 1:7 NKJV

Fear and love do not exist in the same place, just as light and darkness cannot coexist. They directly oppose one another. Yet fear is something we must deal with every day. Our perspective is limited and human. Fear can be paralyzing and cause us to fail in our godly mandate. It's like a poison that weakens and kills our faith in God. So, it is imperative to remember that God has not given us a spirit of fear. The spirit he gives us is one of power, love, and a sound mind.

The reason for these particular attributes is because fear cannot exist where these three are present. When we stand in the power of God, we know that there is nothing to fear. Also, the Bible tells us that "perfect love casts out fear" (1 John 4:18) because love does not allow the torment of fear. Finally, when we have a sound mind, we can see things clearly and with eternity in mind, which banishes irrationality and fear.

*Lord, fear attacks me, and its crippling effects can make me cower. But your Spirit is never afraid. Help me to overcome spiritual resistance, so that I can charge forward in faith, looking to you for love and direction.*

# FIGHT FOR YOU

*"The Lord will fight for you,*
*and you have only to be silent."*
Exodus 14:14 esv

Imagine a little girl in elementary school. She's timid and often picked on. Since she is afraid and shy, she does not often stand up for herself. Then one day, an older classmate confronts the bullies and tells them to leave her alone. From then on, whenever the little girl faced an attack, that older classmate was there to protect her and fight her battles for her.

Isn't it reassuring to know that God fights our battles for us? He knows we are incapable of protecting ourselves against the devil and his schemes, so he steps in and saves the day again and again. He does so because he loves us, and he only asks for love in return. Life is overwhelming at times, and the enemy looks for any opportunity to attack us. But we needn't worry. All we need to do is run to God and silently watch as he crushes anything threatening us. God knows what we need even before we call, and he is ready to win every battle we face.

*Father, thank you for taking up my fight and saving me. When I am overwhelmed, I will call upon you and then be still. Thank you for your steadfast love and care.*

# PERFECT PEACE

*You will keep in perfect peace*
*all who trust in you,*
*all whose thoughts are fixed on you!*
ISAIAH 26:3 NLT

Anxiety and worry plague us every day. For some of us, that's all we know. When our thoughts are on this world and its troubles, we worry and fret, but all that that does is to stress us out and cause us to doubt. On the other hand, when we fix our thoughts on God and decide to trust him instead, he fills us with a peace that supersedes all the comfort and security found in the world.

Peace that comes from God alone is the sort of peace that equips the beneficiary with the ability to handle anything thrown at her. Even in the darkest part of the fiercest storm, we are not shaken. Our security and peace comes from God, who is bigger than this world. This verse tells us that we will be kept in perfect peace—a peace that surpasses all our human understanding—if we trust in the Lord. Fix your thoughts on God. You will experience not just peace, but perfect peace. It doesn't get any better than that.

*Lord, you tell me that you will keep all who trust in you in perfect peace. With my thoughts fixed on you and all my cares cast away, Lord, may your perfect peace surround and overtake me, so that the world may see your work in me.*

# GODLY WISDOM

*The wisdom from above is first pure, then peaceable, gentle,*
*open to reason, full of mercy and good fruits, impartial and sincere.*
JAMES 3:17 ESV

It is good to know how flawless the wisdom from above truly is. With all the conflicting voices in our culture and lives today, it can be difficult to know what to believe. James provides us with a test to judge if wisdom comes from God. He gives us an in-depth, multisided view of wisdom so that we can recognize it. With this wisdom as our base, we have a starting point for analyzing the rest of the world's claims and opinions.

It is "first pure." James gives us good reason to believe that there is no imperfection to be found in God's Word. This is the way it should be, as words spoken by God will reflect the perfect purity and righteousness of the speaker. In God's Word and in God himself, we have a pure, undefiled wisdom from which to understand the rest of life.

*How good it is, oh Lord, to have a foundation of truth. Teach me to walk in wisdom and not foolishness. Teach me to stand apart from the rest of this world as a person who listens to my God.*

# SHIELD OF FAITH

*In all circumstances take up the shield of faith,*
*with which you can extinguish all the flaming darts of the evil one.*
EPHESIANS 6:16 ESV

Just as a shield was key accessory to a soldier in ancient Rome, so is our faith to us today. We never know when the enemy will try to attack us or break us down, so we must remain vigilant in our faith. The shield of faith is a big component to fighting and winning against the devil's onslaught. Without our faith, we are vulnerable, weak, and flawed humans. We're easy prey.

It is God who makes us strong, for he alone who can overcome the enemy. Therefore, in all circumstances, we must take up our shields and stand ready to use them by remaining in the Word, in prayer, and by staying attentive to what our Lord is saying.

*The attacks of the evil one against me can be hot, fiery, and relentless. Please grant me the strength and perseverance I need to withstand him. Keep my faith intact to shield me from the devil's arrows. Thank you for your Word and guidance, today and every day.*

# JOY OF THE LORD

*"Go your way, eat the fat and drink sweet wine and send portions of them to those for whom nothing is prepared, for this day is holy to our Lord; and do not be grieved, for the joy of the Lord is your strength."*

NEHEMIAH 8:10 NRSV

Joy and strength are two attributes with a connection that might not be immediately apparent. Rarely do we see the two listed together. When we take the time to consider, we realize that it truly does take incredible strength to be joyful in all circumstances.

This particular verse was given to Israel when the law was reestablished by the prophet Nehemiah after Israel had fallen captive. They had returned home and were facing many difficult situations. Times were hard, and the strength they needed to pull through was found in the joy of the Lord. Instead of focusing on their struggles, they could focus on the Lord, and he would strengthen them to be able to overcome the days ahead. The same principle applies to us today. God's joy is what enables us to overcome hardships and tough situations. Indeed, God's joy is our strength.

*God, thank you for the joy you give. It strengthens me to keep pressing on, even when things are tough. I choose to focus on you and to be glad in you.*

# SEEK AND FIND

*"You will seek me and find me
when you seek me with all your heart."*
JEREMIAH 29:13 NIV

Life offers us plenty of pursuits: happiness, wealth, power, fame, and more. Only one pursuit truly fulfills the human soul: the pursuit of the one who fashioned and formed each and every human soul.

Only God can satisfy us fully and forever because he was the one who made us, and he made us for himself. The Lord knows our hearts perfectly and can satisfy each longing we have and every purpose we seek. If we seek him wholeheartedly, we will find him. He doesn't ask us to travel to the ends of the earth, learn perfect theology, or act perfectly all the time. He simply wants us to honestly and completely seek him.

*Lord, thank you for the revelation that whoever seeks after you in earnest will find you. Help me to be a seeker of your will and your purpose in my life, all day and every day, to the glory of your name.*

# UNDESERVED LOVE

*"If anyone slaps you on one cheek,*
*offer him the other cheek, too.*
*If someone takes your coat,*
*do not stop him from taking your shirt."*

LUKE 6:29 NCV

The Bible asks us what credit it is to us if we are kind to good people and give to those who we know will return good for good. Anyone can do that. The harder thing to do is to be kind to the cruel and generous to the poor. When people see us behaving in this way, it stands out to them because there is no selfish motive or expectation of reward.

This kind of love is what our Father has for us. He sent his Son to die for our sins. How can we claim to be redeemed if we withhold that love from others? God loved us when we were still trapped in our sins, so we also should love others without condition. To love the undeserving is to practice the will of God.

*Please, open my eyes to the opportunities you give me each day to love others in the way you love me, Father, with joy and compassion. May I be so grateful for your compassion and love that I can't help but share it with others.*

# REDEEMED WITH PURPOSE

*You are a chosen generation, a royal priesthood, a holy nation,*
*His own special people, that you may proclaim the praises of Him*
*who called you out of darkness into His marvelous light.*

1 PETER 2:9 NKJV

Peter says that we are a "chosen race, a royal priesthood, a holy nation, a people for his own possession" (ESV). What a wonder it is to be chosen! Not by accident, but with planning and consideration, we were chosen to be children of God. This verse shows us the intimate, unbreakable connection between God and us, his own people.

Our transformation into God's people leads us to praise and testify about God. Peter says that we were chosen to "proclaim the excellencies of him who called you out of the darkness." The light of Christ shone among us so that we could tell others of its brightness. There is no amount of darkness that can stop us from proclaiming the excellencies of God's marvelous light. After all, no amount of sin kept God from choosing us.

*Lord, it is an incredible gift to be chosen. We are forever a people marked by the light of your grace. Today, may I proclaim your excellencies and shine your light. May all around me see my testimony and therefore look to you.*

# COURAGE AND STRENGTH

*So be strong and courageous,*
*all you who put your hope in the LORD!*
PSALM 31:24 NLT

There will be times in life when we want to give in to despair. Upsetting situations happen to us all. We, however, have a hope that is unshakable. We have courage and strength to make it through the bleakest of days, because our hope is in a God who never fails and never disappoints. Although the seasons of our lives may change—from bad to good and back again—the faithfulness and love of God is everlasting. Knowing that he will never leave us equips us with the bravery we need to face dark days.

We are not removed from the world's problems because we follow God. Problems will come regardless. The difference is that we have a clear path forward and the power of God on our side, making us strong enough to face every obstacle with confidence and courage.

*Lead me, dear Jesus, and renew my hope daily. When I am weak, you surround me with your care and prove that you are strong enough to weather the storms. I cling to you, and you make me courageous!*

# INSTRUCTIONS AND COUNSEL

*I will instruct you and teach you the way you should go;*
*I will counsel you with my eye upon you.*

PSALM 32:8 NRSV

The Lord Almighty is eager to share his many mysteries with us. Like us, he desires to be known, understood, pursued, and enjoyed. There are so many secrets he willingly and readily reveals to those who seek him and want a close relationship with him. Our Lord shares all things with his friends. He teaches and instructs us, guiding us through a complicated world.

Whenever we feel lost or confused, we can turn to our Father's welcoming arms and understanding smile. In his Word is the counsel and direction we need to make wise decisions and find our way through. He is our Father: the perfect teacher, counselor, and comforter. He watches us with compassion and never, ever looks away. His eyes are always upon us, keeping us safe and enjoying our company.

*You have taught me so many things, Father God. You hold the answers that I seek. Truly, it is you I am seeking, and when I do, everything else starts to make sense. Thank you for sharing yourself and your creation with me.*

# GROWING THROUGH ADVERSITY

*We also have joy with our troubles, because we know that these
troubles produce patience. And patience produces character,
and character produces hope.*

ROMANS 5:3-4 NCV

The difference between those who know God and those who
refuse to know him is not found in the ease of life, but in conviction
and focus. All of us experience adversity from time to time, but
Christians understand that troubles produce patience, which
produces character, which leads to hope. Because of our hope, we
have joy in the face of the most terrible of circumstances. We see
beyond our temporary situations and to the fulfillment of God's
promises.

Instead of diminishing our love, trials grow it. Rather than lose
hope, hardships strengthen it. More and more we learn that this life
is not what we live for, because God has made us for so much more.
When others are down, we keep our eyes up and help them find
the hope we are already resting in.

*Help me grow through my adversity, God, and learn to
hope in you. Give me patience and perspective. Please, grow
my character as I learn to live for you and not this life only.*

# REST

*All who have entered into God's rest have rested from their labors, just as God did after creating the world.*

HEBREWS 4:10 NLT

Because of our constant state of busyness, we are always looking for rest. We try taking a week off work, sleeping in, changing jobs, but nothing works. If we can't learn to rest during our busy seasons, we will always be waiting for the next new thing to bring us peace, and we will never actually attain it.

We have the power to rest in the middle of hectic schedules and late nights by seeking God and asking him to make our hearts still. We can walk with God throughout the day, talking to him and praying to him, and experience rest by giving him control, trusting him to take care of us. After all, he was the one who created rest. He was the first to experience it on that seventh day of creation.

*Lord, teach me how to rest in you. Show me how to give you authority in my life. Help me stop worrying about the details. Please, forgive me for the times I try to create my own rest instead of seeking you.*

# TOGETHER WITH HIM

*If we are joined with him in his sufferings,*
*then we will reign together with him in his triumph.*
*But if we disregard him, then he will also disregard us.*
2 TIMOTHY 2:12 TPT

Paul looks at the difficulties which we are asked to endure, and he gives us two reasons to continue. Firstly, there is the promise of reigning with our Savior after our life is past. Secondly, there is a warning that references Luke 12:9: "The one who denies me before men will be denied before the angels of God" (ESV). Paul is reminding us that we sought salvation because we were cut off from God, separated from his true love for us. To deny him now would be to throw away all that we gained. It would be to count the struggles of a small lifetime as not worthy of the glory of eternity.

We cannot forget the first promise in light of the second one. Christ is on our side, cheering for our success, awaiting the moment when he can crown us in his new kingdom. He is not expecting to punish us. He plans on granting us joy for the sake of his righteousness, which lives inside of us.

*Christ Jesus, there is every reason to press on to the finish. Keep my eyes centered on the glory that lies ahead. Keep my mind on the promises you have given me. Today, in humble glory, may I persevere by your strength and will. Thank you, Lord.*

# A TIME FOR EVERYTHING

*A time to seek, and a time to lose;
a time to keep, and a time to cast away.*
ECCLESIASTES 3:6 NRSV

Can you remember a time when the Lord blessed you with something, but later it was taken from you? The direction of life may change, or we may need to let go of something or someone we love. In everything, the love of God is constant and assured. Even in the face of loss, we can know for certain that everything God does is out of love. He may be asking you to let go of something or to trust him after it was already ripped away. There is a time for everything in this life, but in the life to come, there will no longer be loss. A day is coming when we will never need to endure the sting of death or distress again.

For now, as long as our lives continue, seasons will change, and our only firm foundation is to stand on the promises of God. Through loss and gain, poverty and wealth, rejection and love, the one thing we can always count on is that God will be there, ready to hold our hands.

*In every season, Father God, I trust you. Regardless of what happens, you are fully reliable and true to your character. I stand on your Word, knowing that I cannot be shaken.*

# CHRIST'S YOKE

*"Take my yoke upon you.*
*Let me teach you, because I am humble and gentle at heart,*
*and you will find rest for your souls."*

MATTHEW 11:29 NLT

Here, Christ says to take his yoke and learn from him. This is discipleship. We can read a hundred books on how to be a better Christian, but none of them will replace the value of walking and learning directly from Christ on a personal level. He does not want us know things about him; he wants us to know him. This is his ultimate plan for our lives, one which will glorify him and us.

Christ also promises that our souls will find rest. Being under God's yoke does not mean laboring and toiling with nothing to revive our spirits. We will labor, this is true, but only while being sustained through Christ. We can only learn how to work in God's power and gain rest for our souls by leaning into his Word, his voice, and his teachings.

*Christ Jesus, today is a day of discipleship. It is a day where I should walk with you, learn from you, and seek after you. Put upon me your easy yoke and let me learn to know you.*

# HIS COVENANT STANDS

*My covenant I will not break,*
*Nor alter the word that has gone out of My lips.*
PSALM 89:34 NKJV

Can you remember a time you have been lied to or betrayed? Do you recall the feelings that this experience created in you? Have you ever let someone else down or broken a promise? Each of us has failed to follow God's laws from time to time. We have all hurt him with our behavior and our choices, yet he stays constant and unyielding in his love and loyalty toward us.

"If we are faithless, he remains faithful; he cannot deny himself" (2 Timothy 2:13). No matter how wretchedly or unworthily we act, he will love us and accept us back every time we come running. His covenant will never break because he is faithful and true. What he has spoken, he will do. It is up to us to decide if we will disregard his grace or strive to learn from his example, growing in our love and loyalty to him.

*You are so good, Lord God. And your goodness teaches me how I ought to act. I hope to never take your graciousness for granted. I want to grow in my own faithfulness and godly behavior.*

# LOOK FORWARD TO

*How abundant are the good things
that you have stored up for those who fear you,
that you bestow in the sight of all,
on those who take refuge in you.*

PSALM 31:19 NIV

Isn't it heart-warming to know that God is preparing heaven for us? He has good things waiting for the ones who abide in him and are not ashamed of his name. It can be helpful to remember that this hard journey called life is not forever. We are working toward a greater purpose: a beautiful, worshipful, heavenly kingdom. When all the pain and the suffering is over, peace will reign.

It's easy to complain about our struggles and feel weighed down by the world. When we can see the end goal and worship God through hardship, that is when he is glorified, and it is when others see him through us.

*Father, I am grateful that you are my support in this life. I know that you have a place ready for me when it is over. Thank you for giving me these promises to look forward to and for helping me share this good news with the world.*

# INSPIRED BY THE WORLD

*Do not be fooled:*
*"Bad friends will ruin good habits."*
1 CORINTHIANS 15:33 NCV

Our environment has a great effect on who we become. When we are willingly in an environment that is bad—opposed to God—then our soul will begin to wander away God. This is the reason why Paul so adamantly tells the Corinthians not to be deceived. There is no room for error when running either toward or away from God, and our direction is influenced by the company we keep.

Paul never intended for God's people to close themselves off from "bad" people. He also did not think it impossible to be good in an evil culture, an evil environment, or an evil nation. However, if we rely upon, trust in, and relax with poor company, then we are not living with Christ in our minds. The bad company of this world is our mission field.

*Only by your power can I live among bad company and not become like them, Father God. Make me into a witness for your glory, unshaken by the powers of darkness all around me. Let my morals be inspired by my good company of fellow believers, unshaken by the world of evil.*

# SEEK ADVICE

*Without consultation, plans are frustrated,*
*But with many counselors they succeed.*
PROVERBS 15:22 NASB

People are very smart. Most of us know someone, or many people, who are not only knowledgeable about the way the world works, but also wise in the ways of the Scriptures. There is always someone who knows more than us. These are the people we should seek out for advice. They are people we trust: people that we've seen make mistakes and recover, while trusting God the whole time. The best plan anyone could make on their own could always be improved by wisdom from someone who has experience pertaining to the subject.

When Jesus finished his time on earth, he didn't pass on the responsibility of spreading the gospel to just one person, but to many. He knew that between their different perspectives and experiences, they could challenge each other and reach a conclusion much closer to the truth than if they were thinking on their own.

*God, I pray that you would put individuals in my life who know you and can help me to honor you. I also pray that you would prepare me, so that I can give advice to someone who needs it.*

# EVERY WORD

*"I tell you, on the day of judgment you will have to give an account for every careless word you utter; for by your words you will be justified, and by your words you will be condemned."*

MATTHEW 12:36-37 NRSV

Jesus lovingly healed a demon-possessed man, and the Pharisees immediately started in with their accusations. Their ignorant and hateful words betrayed their true desire to persecute and condemn Jesus. They hated his message that contradicted their own way of living, so they sought to find fault in him however they could. In response to their indictments, Jesus cautioned them that they would one day have to answer for every word they spoke.

Those who are ready to condemn others may find themselves condemned in the end. God alone is the judge, the only one qualified to pass judgment and condemnation on others.

*Guard my mouth, Lord. May my words always reflect your love in my heart. You know my thoughts and the words my heart whispers. You forgave me when I deserved condemnation, so I will not cast judgment or hatred on others.*

# RESTORATION

*He heals the brokenhearted
and bandages their wounds.*
PSALM 147:3 NLT

The world we live in is so lost and broken, it tries to cover its grief and find relief in anything other than God. Rather than simply asking the Lord for help or finding comfort in his Word, people run to temporary fixes like alcohol, sex, drugs, affirmation from others, social media, entertainment, or food. Some hide their pain behind a wall of coldness or comedy. Many are prone to isolation.

Attempting to survive without the healing power of Jesus can only be a temporary coping mechanism, allowing bitterness and despondency to spread. Giving our grief to God is the only way to truly heal, for he is a perfect physician who heals the brokenhearted and bandages up wounds. In him, we find our hope and freedom. By his mercy, we endure.

*Jesus, I reach out for your healing hand. Thank you for your relief and your comfort, and for not leaving me alone in my heartache.*

# FALSE PROPHETS

*Do not believe every spirit, but test the spirits, whether they are of God; because many false prophets have gone out into the world.*

1 JOHN 4:1 NKJV

We have all witnessed the mismanagement of Scripture. All too often, the Bible is misused for the betterment of the speaker, rather than for the relationship between the Lord and the hearer. False prophets are a problem today, and they were a problem in Jesus' day as well. Marketing brilliance or on-brand messaging don't matter, especially if the words spoken are not true and not for the glory of God alone.

The Word of God brings clarity and peace, not guilt and offense. We can test the messages we hear and the spirits that try to influence us by aligning them with the heart of God. The King we serve is benevolent, loving, and forgiving. Those who oppose his message and example of love are not those who speak the truth. When we know God intimately, we will be able to identify his true messengers from those who are self-seeking and false.

*Teach me your ways, Lord. Reveal yourself to me, so that I may love you and serve you to the best of my ability. Please, give me discernment to know what things are of you and what should be disregarded. You are my source of truth and wisdom.*

# ALL THINGS

*We are convinced that every detail of our lives is continually woven together to fit into God's perfect plan of bringing good into our lives, for we are his lovers who have been called to fulfill his designed purpose.*

ROMANS 8:28 TPT

What God considers good is not what most people consider good. If we are taught to depend on God under great tribulation, believing ourselves to be burdened beyond our own strength, then God considers it good. More than that, he considers it our good. The circumstances are bad, but they are working for our good.

Being blessed is hard to define, mostly because we are often most blessed by the struggles that bring us closer to God. On the other hand, times of rest do wonders for our spiritual renewal. Somehow, God manages to use these diverse circumstances for our ultimate benefit and his glory.

*God, somehow you have made today to be to my benefit. You have made the daily doldrum, the struggles, and the joys to further mold me into your image. May I recognize this and give you praise for it.*

# THE SPIRIT HELPS US

*In the same way the Spirit also helps our weakness; for we do not know what to pray for as we should, but the Spirit Himself intercedes for us with groanings too deep for words.*

ROMANS 8:26 NASB

Sometimes, we think we need something, but it will actually impede us. On our own, how can we know what we need, since the future is unknown to us? Perhaps we think we need more strength when what we actually need is rest. Or perhaps we think we need more money when what we really need is to slow down and be content. Maybe we think we need a different job, but what will truly help us is an opportunity for clearer communication at work.

Whatever discontent we're experiencing, our Father knows what we need when we do not. His Spirit stays with us to help us, since we are like children who do not know the best way to pray. He intercedes for us and helps us in our weaknesses. He understands that our understanding is finite and makes allotments for our humanity. Praise God for his wisdom!

*It is for my sake that you sent your Spirit, Almighty God. Thank you for not giving me everything I think I need and instead taking care of me in the best way, like a true and good father.*

# SEPTEMBER

"Humanly speaking, it is impossible.
But with God everything is possible."

MATTHEW 19:26 NLT

# A NEW THING

*"Behold, I am doing a new thing;*
*now it springs forth, do you not perceive it?*
*I will make a way in the wilderness*
*and rivers in the desert."*

ISAIAH 43:19 ESV

The prophet Isaiah recorded many of God's reminders to the people of Israel. They readily forgot his miracles and abandoned his ways, so he constantly reminded them of who he was and what he had down for them, proving that he was worthy of their praise and worship. When the Israelites were fleeing from their Egyptian captors, it was the Lord who separated the seas and made a way through for them. When they were thirsty and starving in the desert, he provided food and water. When they drifted and started worshipping false gods, he sent prophets to remind them of the truth.

Most importantly, however, when we were all lost to sin with no hope of redemption, he sent his Son, Jesus Christ, to make a way for us: a way in the wilderness. This is the "new thing" he was doing.

*You are a life-giving river in a dry and difficult desert, Lord. I praise you for all you have done on my behalf to lead me, love me, and keep me safe.*

# ACT FAITHFULLY

*Lying lips are an abomination to the LORD,*
*but those who act faithfully are his delight.*
PROVERBS 12:22 NRSV

The devil is the father of lies; that is the only language he knows. When we lie, we are participating in the language of the enemy. As followers of Christ and proclaimers of the truth, we should always endeavor to keep our lips from lying. When we slip up, rather than concoct more lies to cover it up, we can lessen the damage by telling the truth and looking to the Lord for forgiveness. No matter the cost, it is necessary to speak the truth because the truth will set us free.

James points out that a spring doesn't pour forth from the same opening both fresh and brackish water. Likewise, how can believers mix truth with lies? If we are indeed children of the truth, then we cannot follow the rhetoric of the liar.

*You called me to yourself and set me apart from the world. Please, give me boldness and unwavering faith to stand in the truth, regardless of the pressures or gain to lie.*

# SCRIPTURES

*Using the Scriptures, the person who serves God will be capable,
having all that is needed to do every good work.*

2 TIMOTHY 3:17 NCV

The Scriptures are an essential part of every believer's life and development. They are the very words of God and how we learn from him. They reveal God's will and give us divine guidance. The more we learn the Word of God, the better we understand who he is and what his desires are. The Bible's wisdom is an indispensable part of our daily lives, teaching and equipping us for every good work. The Scriptures are a Christian's tool of trade; without them, every task we are given is more difficult. They are our roadmap, keeping us from getting lost.

As an irreplaceable, integral part of our journey, it is so important that we continue to find time in our daily lives to read the Bible and learn its wisdom. Our lives, and the lives of those around us, will reap the rewards of the good works which come more naturally to someone who's walking in the light of Christ.

*How I love your Word, dearest Lord! Through it, all things make more sense. It is my compass that points me back to you.*

# RESPONSIBLE AND FLEXIBLE

*A man's heart plans his way,*
*But the Lord directs his steps.*
PROVERBS 16:9 NKJV

God doesn't always tell us exactly what we should do. He equips us with wisdom and understanding and prepares us through our experiences. Often, we must choose which path to take. Whether choosing between two job opportunities or deciding upon a house for our family, there is often no right or wrong answer. We have the power to make decisions for ourselves, and God has the authority to change them.

We should be responsible for making choices in life while remaining flexible to the many opportunities that God might present to us. We can't be so fixated on our own plans that we are unable to trust God when he calls us to halt what we're doing and follow his lead.

*God, you are all-knowing. I have peace in the knowledge that you are watching over me and guiding me. Please, open my eyes to notice when you are leading me in a new direction, and open my heart to be receptive to your leadership.*

# GOD'S LOVE

*"God so loved the world that he gave his one and only Son,
that whoever believes in him shall not perish but have eternal life."*
JOHN 3:16 NIV

We can accurately measure our love for someone by how much we are willing to lose for them. Long distance relationships know this to be true from the start. In God's case, he was willing to lose the life of his Son for our salvation. He was willing to sacrifice himself because of the love he has for us. If love is measured by sacrifice, then God's love has no limit.

The Lord's love for us is only one part of the verse, however. It is followed by why God sent his Son: that we may believe in him. It is not just pardon from punishment, but acceptance into eternal life by faith. We are given the choice of being part of God's family for all eternity, so why would we say no?

*Lord, you desired my salvation so much you sacrificed your Son. You loved this broken world in a way that no one else could. Open my eyes to the greatness of your love, and may I praise it forevermore.*

# ENTERTAINING ANGELS

*Do not neglect to show hospitality to strangers,*
*for thereby some have entertained angels unawares.*
HEBREWS 13:2 ESV

Middle Eastern weather can be quite inhospitable. It is very dry and hot, which would have made it especially difficult on travelers back in Biblical days, as many walked on foot for kilometers or used pack animals. It became a necessary cultural practice to be hospitable towards strangers who came your way and were in need.

The Bible records several significant encounters that transpired from these interactions. There were even cases where the strangers ended up being angels sent from God! Rebecca showed gracious hospitality to a simple servant who, unbeknownst to her, was waiting for such a sign from God to select a wife for Isaac. Whether it leads to entertaining angels, finding a husband, or simply sharing God's love with someone else, the importance of the biblical mandate to be hospitable cannot be underestimated.

*Father, grant me the heart and the means to be hospitable to people around me, those I know and those who are strangers. I don't want to miss out on the blessings of being a good neighbor and host, because in doing so, we bring glory to your name.*

# LOVE AND AFFECTION

*Love each other with genuine affection,*
*and take delight in honoring each other.*
ROMANS 12:10 NLT

How does the Bible's definition of love differ from the world's perception of what love is? God, who is the originator of love and therefore the true standard, decreed that love should be accompanied with a genuine affection for one another. In a society that expresses love as lust and desire in the media, we need to learn to be pure and true.

We ought to honor others, not simply care about them because of what they can offer us. That sort of love is self-seeking and disingenuous, but the love Christ showed us and filled us with is authentic and unbreakable. With this love, we can embrace others with a pure expression of affection and become more like Christ.

*Christ Jesus, instill in me real, genuine love. I want my love to be defined by you, not by what the world perceives love to be. Help me to be generous and delight in others. I pray that those around me stop to notice that I am changed because of the work you have done within me.*

# FAITHFUL TO THE END

*I pray with great faith for you, because I'm fully convinced that the One who began this glorious work in you will faithfully continue the process of maturing you and will put his finishing touches to it until the unveiling of our Lord Jesus Christ!*

PHILIPPIANS 1:6 TPT

The Bible reveals the return our Lord Jesus Christ and tells us to prepare ourselves. We all sin, and none of us are worthy to stand before our Maker. Rather than being afraid or trying to cover up our failure, our best move is to humbly fall before our Father and open our hearts to accept his glorious work. He will heal our hearts, convict us of our sin, strengthen us to overcome, and lead us to victory, if we submit to him and allow his process of maturing to take place.

Until the very end, our Lord God is faithful to finish what he has started. We cannot accomplish this on our own, but we most certainly can rely on the healing power and process of God.

*God, you have a plan already in place for me. You have laid a path for me to follow, and you promise to walk with me every step of the way. Thank you for healing me. Continue to completion what you have already started in me.*

# PERFECTED IN WEAKNESS

*"My grace is sufficient for you, for power is perfected in weakness."*
*Most gladly, therefore, I will rather boast about my weaknesses,*
*so that the power of Christ may dwell in me.*

2 CORINTHIANS 12:9 NASB

Paul had a figurative thorn in his flesh, and he prayed to God to remove it. Instead, God's solution was to use this hardship as a way to demonstrate to Paul that his grace was sufficient. Paul did not need to be strong enough to take on the world, because God was going to do it through him.

God's power is limitless! The paradoxical way God chooses to work though the weaknesses, pains, and failures of humanity is an inspiring testimony of redemption and a way for him to prove his power to the world. We cannot boast in our own strength when we recognize our own weaknesses and limitations. Instead, we can humbly allow the greatness of Christ working in and through us to be obvious to all. When we suffer from our own thorns and restrictions, we can start to see them as opportunities to showcase God's love and power to the world around us.

*I want to be humble and trust you, Lord God. Remind me and show me how your grace is enough in every situation and in my weaknesses.*

# WASTED TIME

*A thousand years in your sight*
*are like a day that has just gone by,*
*or like a watch in the night.*
PSALM 90:4 NIV

Time holds no control over God, but it is not so with us. We live in time, surrounded by the reality of growing old and either missing or taking advantage of opportunities. What we do with our time is decided by how we view it, since "a thousand years in [God's] sight are but as yesterday when it is past" (ESV). This is not how people want to think of time, though. We would like to think that the glories of our earthly life last forever, or that trials and pain are far too long to endure.

Our relationship with God reconciles us to the thought that our time will end. Christ gives us something of eternal importance to do. We can be the hands and feet of Jesus in our limited time, our watch in the night. While we will pass from existence sooner than we realize, what we do through faith in Christ can last forever.

*Only you reign freely over time itself, Lord. No one else sees humankind's toiling and futility as completely as you do. By your grace, let me not be forgotten once I have passed from this earth. Help me spend my time in a way that has eternal significance.*

# SHIELD OF SALVATION

*"You have also given me the shield of Your salvation;*
*your gentleness has made me great."*
2 SAMUEL 22:36 NKJV

The imagery of a shield depicts a battle. Someone who needs a shield is under attack. For a Christian, there is a battle raging every day in the spiritual realm. We live contrary to the world's systems and the devil's agenda, so we are guaranteed to meet opposition. That is why the Bible warns us to wear the full armor of God (Ephesians 6:10-18). The worst things happen to a soldier when she is unprepared. Indeed, walking into a battle underdressed is a recipe for disaster!

The spiritual battle around us is real and constant, so we must stay vigilant. Equipped with our shields of faith, just as David did in this verse, we can stand firm in the truth that has been revealed to us. The same Lord who prepared David for battle and gave him his shield also prepares us. It is God's gentleness that makes us great, and he will equip us to win the battle.

*I am constantly at war against the devil's schemes, the world's evil ploys, and against my own sinful nature, God. I need your gentleness to help me overcome and your salvation to shield me. Thank you for generously granting both.*

# EMPATHY

*They sat on the ground with him for seven days and seven nights. No one said a word to him, because they saw how great his suffering was.*
JOB 2:13 NIV

To empathize with someone is to understand or identify with their situation. It is the ability to put yourself in their shoes and share their pain. Empathy is not an easy characteristic to personify, because it means intentionally leaving our blissful naivety and embracing someone else's suffering. It requires us to cast aside our own comfort and partake in the discomfort and pain of others. We may pity others or show sympathy to their plight, but to actually sit in the dirt with another, to cry with them and embody their hurts, takes true love.

Rather than leaving us to wallow in our sin and receive the death penalties we deserve, Jesus Christ empathized with us. Nobody can say that he does not understand what they are going through, because he took all the brokenness of the world in his own body and suffered on our behalf. Rather than stay in our comfortable lives, let's follow the example of Christ, empathize with the hurting, and sit on the ground with them while they cry. Empathy is important in the life of every believer in order to cultivate a life that reflects the love of Christ.

*God, you know how self-centered I can be, how I fail to see others in need. Open my eyes and heart to see others the way you do. May I be a representation of you by going the extra mile and giving myself.*

# VICTORIOUS IN CHRIST

*We thank God! He gives us the victory through our Lord Jesus Christ.*
1 CORINTHIANS 15:57 NCV

The greater context of this verse is overcoming sin and death through Christ Jesus. He stands victorious over death, and he extends his victory to us, his followers. Since the first sin was ever committed, everyone has experienced the crushing blows of sin, suffering, and death. Every single day, we writhe under the stronghold of a cursed world, chains around our necks.

But thanks to Christ's ultimate sacrifice, we are not in bondage to this world or its curses anymore. We may feel the weight of them for some time until Christ returns for us, but we are not ruled by them. Their hold on us was shattered, and we are free to walk in the glorious revelation of what God truly intends for his children.

*Thank you, Lord, for your victory over sin and death, which has freed me to live for your kingdom rather than in bondage to this world. I praise you for setting me free from the stranglehold of sin in my life. May all glory and praise be given to you forever!*

# THE BUDDY SYSTEM

*Bear one another's burdens,*
*and thereby fulfill the law of Christ.*
GALATIANS 6:2 NASB

From the Bible's beginning, we see that God does not want people to be alone. He created animals to keep Adam company, but that wasn't enough. God knew animals would not satisfy Adam's loneliness, so he created a counterpart to him, to challenge and to love him.

Community is one of the most important parts of following God because we are all of one body, with Christ at the head. We are not islands, but rather a network of individuals made to sharpen, encourage, and support one another. A lone person can only grow so much without differing perspectives. New and experienced believers need to guide and challenge each other in order to draw closer to God and develop a deeper understanding of his will and plan.

*Lord, when I stumble into the rut of thinking that I am fine on my own, please send people into my life who will help me to learn and grow. May I never grow apathetic or think that I have it all figured out. Instead, remind me to always strive to know you better.*

# LOVE AND DISCIPLINE

*If you do not punish your children, you don't love them,*
*but if you love your children, you will correct them.*
PROVERBS 13:24 NCV

True love is unconditional and seeks the good of others. If we honestly love our children, we will not be complicit in their corruption. To watch them turn away from God with no voice of correction is to hate them, not love them. God has made us a parent in order to steward them while they are in our care, and to bear the responsibility of love and correction.

This proverb encourages us to love our children by mirroring the way God loves us. From experience, people come to see that God afflicts us in order to better us, not destroy us. Similarly, the parent's role is to rebuke when necessary, so that the child can be the person they have the potential of becoming. This will not happen through permissiveness, but through active love and discipline.

*What a responsibility I have, Lord, in being a parent or guardian. Thank you for the rewards it brings. May I arrive at these rewards through faithful stewardship of the little ones that you have placed in my care.*

# CALL TO HIM

*"Call to me and I will answer you,*
*and will tell you great and hidden things*
*that you have not known."*

JEREMIAH 33:3 NRSV

How incredible is this invitation? The Lord God Almighty promises that if we call him, he will answer us. Not only that, but he also says that he will tell us great things. That which was previously hidden to us, he will make known. The scope of this offer portrays both God's powerful omniscience and his heartfelt desire to include us in what he knows and what he is doing. There is so much we don't know that he longs to share with us.

Who could resist this kind of invitation? Who wouldn't want a closer relationship with the loving Father and to realize his hidden mysteries? God told us through the prophet Jeremiah that there are unsearchable wonders beyond our imagination, and all we need to do to discover them is to discover him. Call to him, and he will indeed answer. Know him and partake in his knowledge, because his desire is to share all things with us—his heirs. We cannot fathom what he has in store for those whose hearts search for him.

*Your greatness and wisdom are beyond my comprehension, dear Father. My finite mind cannot grasp all that you are, but you have invited me to get to know you on a deeper level. I accept!*

# NO ONE LIKE GOD

*No one is holy like the LORD!*
*There is no one besides you;*
*there is no Rock like our God.*
1 SAMUEL 2:2 NLT

Hannah was barren in a culture and a time in history when it was shameful for a woman to be unable to bear children. In fact, it was one of the worst disgraces for a woman. It is no surprise that Hannah was in absolute anguish over this situation for many years. To make matters worse, her husband's other wife often mocked Hannah because of her infertility. In time, however, the Lord answered Hannah's cries, and she gave birth to the boy who would become the prophet Samuel.

In today's verse, Hannah is worshipping God for the incredible miracle of a baby. Her adoring praises echo her gratefulness and commitment. There is no one like our God! There is no one as holy nor reliable, as faithful or as loving. He is truly awesome beyond comprehension, and we can never ever truly grasp the fullness of who he is.

*Lord, I am so grateful you are who you are. I can't count the ways you have blessed me. You are good, kind, compassionate, and faithful. You hear me when I cry. There is no rock like you.*

# JESUS IS THE WAY

*"I am the Way, I am the Truth, and I am the Life.
No one comes next to the Father except through union with me.
To know me is to know my Father too."*

JOHN 14:6 TPT

The Old Testament was a series of signs pointing to the coming of the Messiah. He is the way, the truth, and the life prophesied about throughout the entire Scriptures. How could we, as imperfect people, dare go before a perfect God? There is no amount of good works we can do to override our imperfection. We needed a way though, and Jesus came to provide that way. He is the fulfillment of the truth promised from the time the very first sin was committed.

Following Jesus is the only way that leads to life, because nobody is worthy or capable of union with God outside of the grace and forgiveness given to us by Jesus Christ. In fact, we cannot know God outside of Jesus because Jesus is God. To know him is to know the Father also.

*Keep me on your path, King Jesus! I am excited to follow your truth and to find eternal life. Thank you for your continued guidance.*

# STRENGTH IN WEAKNESS

*That is why, for Christ's sake, I delight in weaknesses,*
*in insults, in hardships, in persecutions, in difficulties.*
*For when I am weak, then I am strong.*
2 CORINTHIANS 12:10 NIV

We know that the little strength we have is nothing compared to God's power. That can make us feel inadequate, but God tells us that our weaknesses are exactly what he uses in order to show us his glory. God picked Gideon, who was intensely afraid, to free Israel from one of their most powerful captors. He picked Mary, a young unmarried girl, to be the mother of Jesus.

God chooses the lowly because his beauty starkly contrasts our sinful nature. When people see what comes from the holes in our character, they look to find its source. If we were perfect, there would be nothing to fix, and we would have no need for God's saving grace. We can praise God for the pieces of ourselves that we aren't proud of. We know that he is going to use them to show us his power.

*God, you always have a plan, even for my failures. The things I try to hide are where you most want to work. Please, soften my heart to your will, and give me the strength to give you my weaknesses.*

# SANCTIFIED

*The answer is, if you eat or drink, or if you do anything,*
*do it all for the glory of God.*
1 CORINTHIANS 10:31 NCV

We cannot please God by doing the right things, like getting up early versus sleeping in, or reading the Bible instead of mowing the lawn. There are no actions or behaviors that are especially holy. It is only by doing them for the glory of God that they become acceptable. If we sleep in, let us do so out of a conviction that we need rest, and so do it for the glory of God. If we believe that simply doing something will please God, we are wrong. If we trust in God to purify our actions and make them holy, then the intentions of our hearts are pleasing to God, and as consequence, so are our actions.

God is pleased that he made us unable to do anything on our own. If we could, then glory would be due to us. Instead, God made us helpless creatures. This brings all the glory to God, who is the only one able to help us do everything and hold nothing against us.

*Only you can make me into your righteous child, so I pray for your sanctification this day. God, show me how to entrust my every action to you, bringing glory to you by doing so. May my life today reflect your presence working in me.*

# CLARITY IN BELIEVING

*Whatever you believe about these things keep
between yourself and God. Blessed is the one
who does not condemn himself by what he approves.*
ROMANS 14:22 NIV

Every one of us has an individual relationship with our Maker, and we are each on a unique journey with him. His truths are absolute, but we are not all at the same place of understanding. Whatever we do should be done in faith. If we feel we are sinning and our conscience betrays us, we have indeed sinned. Perhaps we understand that something is permitted for Christians, but a sister or brother has not yet concluded this. We should not push them to go against their conscience, because that would encourage them to go against their faith, and we would be leading them to sin.

Whatever we believe, Romans 14 clearly tells us that our efforts should be towards peace and edification. Let us have grace and patience for those who are not at the same place on their journey as we are, just as the Lord has mercy and grace on us in the face of our own immaturity.

*Lord, please give me wisdom to encourage others and work towards peace. I never want to cause a sister or brother to stumble. Help me to see what people need, dear Father.*

# ALL PLEASURE

*You make known to me the path of life;*
*in your presence there is fullness of joy;*
*at your right hand are pleasures forevermore.*
PSALM 16:11 ESV

The psalmist mentions pleasures forevermore, but these pleasures are not like any of the pleasures of earth. They are far better. They are founded in heaven, in eternity itself, so they last forever. Similarly, they never grow less appealing. They are established in the worship of God.

Where are we searching for pleasure? Do we consider our quiet times of devotion as the boring aspect of our life, which must be balanced with other sorts of enjoyment? If we have a true relationship with Christ, then we will continually be brought to a place where we stand in loving wonder of Jesus Christ's beauty. If we cannot see Christ this way, we might not be seeing him at all.

*Lord Jesus, how beautiful you are! Today, please be my source of joy and contentment. May the pleasures of this life, which come and go, not replace the pleasure I have in knowing you.*

# HIS LIFE FOR OURS

*He died for everyone so that those who receive his new life
will no longer live for themselves. Instead, they will live for Christ,
who died and was raised for them.*

2 CORINTHIANS 5:15 NLT

With our acceptance of the Lord Jesus as King over our lives, we cease to live for our own interests and become members of a bigger, better body of believers. The old is gone and the new has come. We surrender control of our lives to him and he takes charge. Therefore, everything we do is through this new perspective, and we are no longer our own.

Belonging to Christ and his kingdom means we follow his lead. Just as he gave up his life for us, we also give up our lives to his service, knowing that his way is the only one that leads to lasting and fulfilling life. Whatever God has in store for us is far greater than what we could achieve on our own. The goodness of the Lord surpasses all.

*Lord, thank you for the forgiveness of sins at Calvary. Thank you for rescuing me from myself and from the enemy. You raised me from the dead and gave me eternal life. All glory belongs to you forever!*

# HATED

*"If the world hates you,*
*remember that it hated me first."*
JOHN 15:18 NLT

As humans, we want to be liked. We want people to smile when they see us, and we want to be accepted. The Bible promises that if we are in Christ, we are going to make some people upset. And some are going to be more than upset. There will be people that outright hate Christians. The comfort we can take from this is that it means we're headed in the right direction.

The gospel is not comfortable or easy to take on. It's full of hard truths and difficult requests, so people want to run from it. We ought to be attentive, though, to the criticism we receive. Just because people respond negatively to our behavior doesn't always mean we're doing the right thing. We should find wise Christians we trust to take advice from, and if they confront us about something, we can go to the Bible and pray about it.

*God, when others beat me down because of the faith I have in you, help me to stand strong in my faith and stand up for what I believe. I know that your rewards come later, and this suffering will be worth it in the end. Thank you for the suffering you did for me.*

# OUR WORK

*Commit your work to the LORD,*
*and your plans will be established.*
PROVERBS 16:3 NKJV

Our work is a great blessing. God is working through us in our work and through our plans. For this reason, we commonly prioritize working for God over knowing God. It becomes more important to us to do the will of the Lord than to actually be near Jesus Christ, which is a terrible danger. Looking at this situation, the writer of Proverbs 16:3 tells us to dedicate our work to the Lord, and any plans will follow.

By promising that our plans will be established, the writer of this proverb is promising the greatest desire of any person who plans. From the start of any endeavor, the greatest fear is that our plan will be just that: a plan with no fruition. It is tough to see the possibility of something great coming from our plans while also knowing that we don't hold ultimate control over whether it happens. God does, however. He will not just establish our plans; he will inspire them and bring them to completion.

*I can trust only you with my plans, Lord. No one else can guarantee their success. I give you my plan for today, praying for you to breathe life into it in a way I cannot. Inspire, establish, and complete all the plans of my heart, God.*

# ALL PRAISE

*All praise to God, the Father of our Lord Jesus Christ.*
*God is our merciful Father and the source of all comfort.*

2 CORINTHIANS 1:3 NLT

We've all heard the phrase, "All good things come from above", but rarely do we stop to give it thought. The lovely things of life— sunsets, fresh fruit, warmth, spring water—they are all created by God to glorify him. He clothed the world in beauty to be pleasing in his sight. Although we live in a broken version of the original Eden, we catch glimpses of the earth that God has planned for the future. If we look, we can see signs of a coming new earth even in our everyday lives, truly good things that give us hope for the time to come.

God has an incredible paradise in store for those who wait for him, and he is getting it ready for us. When the race has been run and we reach the end of time as we know it, our Father will be there, waiting to welcome us into a life of eternal bliss. Until then, he sprinkles small and large joys throughout our allotted time here, so we can have hope for the future.

*When I get discouraged, Lord, you always have a plan to restore my courage and give me energy to keep going. With a longing heart, I look forward to eternity with you, at peace in your good kingdom. Thank you for showing me just enough to inspire me again.*

# NO DOUBT

*Let him ask in faith, with no doubting,*
*for he who doubts is like a wave of the sea driven*
*and tossed by the wind.*

JAMES 1:6 NKJV

There is nothing on earth that compares to the life God has called us to and wants to bless us with. When we are able to overcome our doubt and live by faith, we will experience a freedom which is not available any other way. Yet we all, admittedly, struggle with doubts.

There is no hope for us unless we anchor ourselves in the Word of God and ask him to hold us with his mighty hand. In his grasp, we will be safe from the crashing waves of life that attempt to drown us and pull us under. Peter stepped out of the boat in faith and began to sink because of doubt, so Jesus reached out and saved him in his mercy. We are not to doubt God, but when we do, he will keep us from drowning, because of his abundant mercy.

*Uphold me, Jesus, and reassure my heart. I often doubt that your ways are best, so I ask for your mercy to help me grow in my faith. Please, remove the doubt from my heart.*

# COME TO PASS

*It is not yet time for the message to come true, but that time is coming soon; the message will come true. It may seem like a long time, but be patient and wait for it, because it will surely come; it will not be delayed.*

HABAKKUK 2:3 NCV

Waiting on the Lord can be difficult, but it is so worthwhile. There are lessons to be learned and a closeness to be obtained that can only be discovered in the grueling process of waiting. Patience is important because God's timing is ideal, and his plan is perfect. He has the end already written, and he has our best in mind.

We sacrifice God's best when we try to take things into our own hands and attempt to rush the process, though it is hard to resist trying. One day, all our waiting will be over, but until that time, we cling to hope and look to God.

*God, I will continue to wait for the fulfillment of your message and for your will in my life. In this age of instant gratification and self-preservation, I trust you with my life and with the timing of things. Please help me to be patient and not lose heart.*

# REAL LOVE

*Love is patient, love is kind. It does not envy,*
*it does not boast, it is not proud.*

1 CORINTHIANS 13:4 NIV

This beautiful love verse holds so history and meaning and deserves to be more than mere seed for wedding sermons. Paul wrote it to the Corinthian church as a direct response to the unloving way they had been conducting themselves. Their living practices had become very self-centered. He was calling them to higher standard of living and warning them against the dangers of pride.

We're not to brag about ourselves or be arrogant. Instead, real love celebrates others and builds them up. Love shows others patience when they are struggling rather than condemning them or misusing their struggles to make us look better. Love is not envious of the success or possessions of others and instead rejoices with them and is happy for them. In essence, love cares about others in a real way and doesn't use other people as a means to benefit ourselves.

*Thank you for loving me, Lord God. Please continue to teach me to love others in a real and honest way.*

# RECONCILE

*"My people who are called by My name humble themselves, and pray
and seek My face, and turn from their wicked ways, then I will hear
from heaven, and I will forgive their sin and will heal their land."*

2 CHRONICLES 7:14 NASB

God is a God of reconciliation. Either he is at peace with things, or
he is not. Nothing is neutral. Oftentimes, people think that God is
no longer concerned with them and will not take account of their
actions. But this verse about the people of Israel is a reminder that
God will take account of our actions. He will judge us, and if he loves
us, he may bring tribulation to turn our focus back to him. In fact, it
is not the trial we should fear, but rather the choice to ignore God.

We should never underestimate the lengths God will go to regain
our hearts and rekindle our love for him. We are mistaken if we
assume that God is apathetic, that he will let us fall away from him,
or that he will neglect the life he has planned for us. After all, he
went so far as to offer his one and only righteous Son so we might
be saved. How dearly must he desire our hearts and lives!

*Lord, forgive my transgressions against you. Help me
to relearn your ways and to return my heart to you. Each
and every day, may I glorify you for being strong enough to
never let me go.*

# OCTOBER

They should be rich in good works and generous to those in need, always being ready to share with others. By doing this they will be storing up their treasure as a good foundation for the future so that they may experience true life.

1 TIMOTHY 6:18-19 NLT

# THINGS ABOVE

*Set your minds on the things that are above,*
*not on the things that are on earth.*
COLOSSIANS 3:2 NASB

As we walk with Christ, it is easy to be distracted by the flashing lights and short-term temptations around us. Even sparkly prizes, which are not in and of themselves wrong, can cause us to wander when they become the fixation of our minds. The Lord created all sorts of wonders that we can enjoy, but our devotion and the pursuits of our hearts are meant for God above all else.

Paul shared with the church that they were expected to set aside things of earthly nature and focus on the divine and glorious. If we become too caught up in earthly things, we can lose our focus and stumble into sin and various maladies. Setting our minds on things above allows us to transcend what is shallow and temporal, and therefore embrace what is heavenly and eternal.

*Lord, help me be eternally minded and not lose sight of what this life is all about. I want to live for you, to the glory of your holy name.*

# LOOK FOR THE ETERNAL

*We do not look at the things which are seen, but at the things which are not seen. For the things which are seen are temporary, but the things which are not seen are eternal.*

2 CORINTHIANS 4:18 NKJV

If this lifetime was all there was, most of us would be dismayed at the realization of our bleak existences. Praise God that he has created a better, brighter kingdom, and we are already citizens! We look forward to a better day, a brighter place, and a new life; there, we will be without pain, heartache, disease, or brokenness. We look forward to a new dispensation, one that Christ will usher in at his return.

This was what Paul was speaking about in his letter to the Corinthian church. He encouraged them, saying, "Even though our outward man is perishing, yet the inward man is being renewed day by day" (2 Corinthians 4:16).

*Lord, I do not look at things that are seen but things that are unseen. Thank you for revealing this to me and giving me an eternal inheritance, which far surpasses any temporary earthly gains.*

# TOGETHER AS ONE

*If one part suffers, every part suffers with it;*
*if one part is honored, every part rejoices with it.*
1 CORINTHIANS 12:26 NIV

Our ears hear which way to go, but we cannot walk there with our ears. Our legs and feet, working in agreement, must bring us there. Our eyes chart the path. All parts work together in harmony. If our knees attempt to do the work of our hands, they will fail and our whole body will suffer, because we need our knees. If we stub a toe, our whole body is instantly aware of it and stops to assess whether we need to take care of it or if we are okay enough to continue.

Paul uses the analogy of a body to describe believers because that is how closely knit we are expected to be. If we become jealous of another person's role in the body and forsake our own role, we harm the body. If we are unaware or uncaring towards the suffering of a fellow Christian, or if we try to live independently apart from the body, we become ineffective and cumbersome to the body and its mission. When we submit ourselves to the purposes of the whole body, work together to help and encourage one another in our God-given roles, and when we love others as much as we love ourselves, then we will be harmonious, healthy, and unstoppable.

*Thank you for my role in your body of believers,*
*dear God. Teach me to live for you and to put others*
*before myself.*

# REAL LOVE

*See, I have written your name on my hand.*
*Jerusalem, I always think about your walls.*
ISAIAH 49:16 NCV

We will never be able to understand the magnitude of, or the reasoning behind, the love that Jesus has for us. Maybe we had a difficult time forgiving someone once, but Jesus, who has never once sinned, forgives us over and over again. He gave his life to free us from the power of darkness. His soul was completely separated from God, taking on all of God's wrath, so that we could be free of guilt and live with him forever.

We cannot pay him back for this amazing gift. Thankfully, he requires nothing of us other than that we follow him. This kind of love is special and unique. Nowhere else in the world can we find such a pure and holy love. And it's ours for free.

*Redeemer, thank you so much for the unconditional love that you give me without reserve. I cannot aspire to earn it, but I commit to honoring you because of it. Your love is my hope for the future. Thanks to you, I can go through each day with a full, thankful heart.*

# GOOD MEDICINE

*A joyful, cheerful heart brings healing
to both body and soul.
But the one whose heart is crushed
struggles with sickness and depression.*
PROVERBS 17:22 TPT

When our spirits draw closer to resembling God's spirit, it does us well. God has promised to sustain and restore us, and part of this involves changing our spirits into healthier versions of what we once were. This deepens our souls and allows us to thrive.

Joy gives us greater happiness than fleeting pleasures, and it also brings deep healing to our minds and bodies. Depression is not a small issue. It affects both our spirits and our bodies as it "dries up the bones." It is a double-edged sword against our well-being, as an unhealthy body and a broken spirit contribute to each other's problems. But from this mire, people can emerge. Even though the task is large, "with God all things are possible" (Matthew 19:26).

*Father, you are the healer of broken spirits. I pray for restoration, that depression would be lifted. I want to see good medicine in my soul and in the souls of the people around me.*

# WHERE YOUR HEART IS

*"Where your treasure is,
there will your heart be also."*
LUKE 12:34 ESV

When we take time to step back and evaluate where we invest our time, our resources, and ourselves, it becomes evident where our priorities lie. What do we spend our days, money, and emotions on? What place does God have in our hearts? Are we ready to forego any other pursuit if he calls us to do so?

God's Word is a priceless treasure that offers life and joy. We live in a time and a place that allows us access to the Holy Scriptures whenever we want. Let us soak in the things that really matter, those that have eternal implications. What else could possibly contend for our dedication and persistence besides a loving relationship with the one true God? He is worthy of our full devotion and our lifelong pursuit.

*You, God, are my purest desire. You excite me more than anything else, and I eagerly search for you as one searches for a treasure. Things of the earth have their appeal. They wink and glisten to catch my eye, but they are dull compared to you. Your light fills my eyes and heart, and I cannot turn away.*

# A GOOD WORD

*Anxiety weighs down the human heart,*
*but a good word cheers it up.*
PROVERBS 12:25 NRSV

Anxiety can attack at any time, and suddenly the whole world is weighing down on our hearts. Things inevitably go wrong, and we find ourselves without the control over our lives that we crave. Sometimes, there is nothing we can do about the situation. The evil one waits and watches, and when we are at our lowest, he attacks! He clouds our vision with anxiety and fear, threatening to overwhelm us.

Instead of suffering alone, these are the moments when we must learn to be vulnerable before God and to reach out to others. Reading the truth in God's Word and hearing encouragement from others can lift us up and disperse the clouds. The Bible tells us not to fear because the Lord is with us in everything (Isaiah 41:10). Other people can pray or laugh with us and help us sort through our anxieties. A word of encouragement is never far away.

*Thank you, Father, for your Word that encourages me and overcomes the works of the evil one. May I always run to you and listen to your advice when I'm discouraged. Surround me with people who will speak words of life to me and give me cheerful words for others.*

# HELD IN HIGH ESTEEM

*Choose a good reputation over great riches;*
*being held in high esteem is better than silver or gold.*
PROVERBS 22:1 NLT

The value of a good reputation cannot be emphasized enough. We live in a society where, more often than not, value is based on success, wealth, and material gain, even when it is acquired in a questionable manner. To many people, the ends justify the means. The lifestyle which ensues from this way of thinking is corrupt and toxic.

Those of us who follow Christ and not the ways of this world must do better. We go that extra mile, not only for our own sakes, but because we understand that what we do and how we do it has a direct impact on our image as believers. A good reputation is worth far more than riches because it may help point someone towards Jesus Christ.

*Lord, I want to follow you and take the high road when faced with decisions that are tempting and may compromise my faith. Thank you for giving me your Spirit to direct and strength me.*

# WHEN YOUR ENEMY FALLS

*Do not rejoice when your enemy falls,*
*And do not let your heart be glad when he stumbles.*
PROVERBS 24:17 NKJV

It is easy to hate or resent things or people that harm us. When we witness harm come upon our enemies, it tends to evoke a sense of vindication and happiness. We may rejoice in their misfortune. However, the Lord God is King and Creator of not only us, but of them as well. His heart is grieved by our misfortune but also by theirs. How can we rejoice when God's creation suffers?

Even when we ourselves were enemies of God, he showed us compassion and stretched out his arm to welcome us into his fold. When our enemies fall, rather than celebrate, let us extend a hand to them the same way God extended his to us.

*Oh God, you loved me while I was still a sinner and extended your love to me. When I was your enemy, you returned hate with love. I want to be like you, so please give me the grace to love my enemies also.*

# BEAUTIFULLY SOVEREIGN

*Yours, LORD, is the greatness and the power*
*and the glory and the majesty and the splendor,*
*for everything in heaven and earth is yours.*
1 CHRONICLES 29:11 NIV

It is good to have a king who is totally good and totally in control. Knowing that God deals kindly with his children, the author of 1 Chronicles shouts out with a voice of praise when he sees that God is the acknowledged Creator and King over all. If anyone should receive recognition for anything, it should be our God who has shown himself perfect in every way. No one else is fit to accept such praise.

What a glorious thing to see that this is really how it is. God does stand wonderfully sovereign over all things. He does deserve praise for all "the greatness and the power and the glory." Let us rejoice that we have a God worth praising, since he is the mighty Creator of all things and the gentle Redeemer of our souls.

*How great you are, Lord! No one can comprehend your majesty and dominion. Thank you for giving me a thousand things to be grateful for. Thank you for being a good father and protector, perfect in power and love.*

# GOD IS THE JUDGE

*God is the only Lawmaker and Judge.*
*He is the only One who can save and destroy.*
*So it is not right for you to judge your neighbor.*
JAMES 4:12 NCV

A lot of attention is given to the judgment and condemnation of others. Media, magazines, and movies are often successful at the expense of someone's embarrassing mistake or misunderstanding. It is easy to pass judgment. It is far more difficult to try to understand things from another's perspective. We are not always successful in this.

Since we are called to live differently from the rest of the world, we should abstain from engaging in its harmful practices, such as casting judgment. Instead, let's set an example of love by how we live our lives in submission to the real judge. Let's bring honor and glory to God by gently instructing and guiding others when they go wrong, rather than further distancing them by smearing their name and assuming the worst about their intentions.

*Whether it is my neighbor, sister, or a celebrity on television, please teach me to resist judging others. Lord Jesus, you have given me discernment, but I don't want to abuse that by looking down on anyone else. They are your creation as well, and you work with each of us individually. Help me to have patience, understanding, and love.*

# FAITHFUL

*"The one who is faithful in a very little thing is also faithful in much; and the one who is unrighteous in a very little thing is also unrighteous in much."*

LUKE 16:10 NASB

Barely having the means for survival, yet being faithful with what we have been given, is an example of excellence and proper stewardship. Even those of us who live comfortably and have financial security should devote all that we have to God and his use. This basic principle of being faithful with whatever we have is both Biblical and natural. It is common to start our young lives with very little—little money, little time, little influence, and more. Over time, if we build on what we have, it is bound to mature. If we are careless with the gifts we have been given, it is difficult to grow.

Progression follows discipline and responsibility. God considers who is using his gifts wisely, and those individuals will be rewarded, whether in earthly or heavenly goods. It does not matter if you have been entrusted with a lot or a little. What matters is that you remain faithful to God and recognize that whatever you have as a gift from him and for his glory.

*Lord, remind me not to pass up small opportunities by failing to be faithful where I am. I want the big things, but they need to grow. Teach me to appreciate the little things that I oversee, even as I continue to grow.*

# WORSHIP

*Oh come, let us worship and bow down;*
*let us kneel before the Lord, our Maker!*
PSALM 95:6 ESV

The Lord created us to worship him. He fashioned our hearts in such a way that we would feel most alive, most fulfilled, and most ourselves when we are praising him. It is our purpose and our joy!

In this psalm, David urges the Israelites to worship the Lord because he is Maker of all. Since he is the one who shaped our hearts, it makes sense that we would long for him above all else. There is something beautiful and marvelous about this exhortation; it fills us with awe and amazement at who God is. We marvel at his goodness and surrender to his glory.

*Lord, I am not my own. I belong to you. Today, I heed the words of King David and worship at your feet. I give you all the praise and glory, and I am grateful for the way you made me. You are my King and my Maker, and my favorite place be is with you, praising your name.*

# BEAUTIFUL

*I praise you, for I am fearfully and wonderfully made.*
*Wonderful are your works; that I know very well.*
PSALM 139:14 NRSV

Not only did God make us in his image, but he also made us with intent and love. We are not accidents. We are children who have been crafted masterfully by the Creator who thinks that we, with all our imperfections, are worth saving. How kindly and selflessly we should love others, knowing that they also have been created in love and in God's image.

As humans, we can forget that Jesus' sacrifice wasn't just for us; it was for the world. Jesus died for so many more than just us, and he desperately loves each one that he created. We are beautiful in his eyes. When we go about our days, we should pay attention to how we think of ourselves and others. Are we looking outwardly like humans, or inwardly like God? Are we looking at the hearts and intrinsic value of God's creation, or judging people based on appearance and bias?

*Lord, thank you for telling me in your Word that I am a purposeful creation. The knowledge that you, the holy God, made me and love me is an overwhelming and precious treasure. I praise you for your unending love.*

# MAGNIFICENT AND SUFFICIENT

*It is not that we think we are qualified to do anything on our own.*
*Our qualification comes from God.*
2 CORINTHIANS 3:5 NLT

We are reminded that nothing accomplished by a person who is mighty in faith is worthy of envy. They completed their task sufficiently and nothing more, and it was not even by their own strength. "Our sufficiency is from God," Paul says. Why do we boast in what God has done through us, or feel any jealousy at how others excel where we do not? Not a single Christian can "claim anything as coming from themselves" when God can use anyone to do anything he intends.

God uses his children as vessels of his sufficiency. He accomplishes tasks through us that we would not be able to do, but he is more than capable. Our response should be one of gratitude, as Christ used us to accomplish some aspect of his plan. What a blessing it is to be utilized by God! Is there any other pursuit more fulfilling than doing the will of Christ?

*Lord, you are my sufficiency and excellency. You are more than I can ever be and greater than I can fathom. Break down my desire to rely on my own strength, for I am insufficient. Today, help me to see everything I do as from you.*

# GOD'S INTENTIONS

*You intended to harm me, but God intended it for good to accomplish what is now being done, the saving of many lives.*
GENESIS 50:20 NKJV

The story of Joseph is truly remarkable. When his brothers sold him into slavery, neither he nor they imagined what his fate would one day be. God can take someone from the absolute bottom to the very top, or the other way around. We cannot let our circumstances determine who we are or who we believe God is. It is not uncommon for God to take an impossible situation and use it to display his glory to the world.

If it ever seems there is no hope left or God has overlooked you, remember that, from our human perspective, we cannot begin to fathom the perfect plan God has in place! Do not grow weary or give up hope. When we are patient and faithful, we will see God's true intentions play out in our lives. What others may intend for harm cannot thwart God's plans to accomplish good in and through us.

*Lord God, in the hard times, when things seem to all be going wrong and I wonder why I must endure hurt and injustices, help me to trust you even more. When it is dark and I want to give way to despair, shine your light on me and help me hold only hope.*

# FAITH

*Faith is confidence in what we hope for
and assurance about what we do not see.*
HEBREWS 11:1 NIV

Our hope in Christ is not a wish or a gamble. We are confident that things will happen exactly as the Bible predicts them. We have a hope so certain that it leads directly to our faith. We do not need to see the future to know the end of the story, because everything has happened to this point exactly as God detailed that it would.

We have faith in the unseen, but not the unknown, because we know God. He has proven himself and his character over and over again for as long as we have existed. Because of him, we have faith to follow him confidently into the future. Our faith is not simply a verbal confession. It is an active and obedient way of living that proves we hope in the Lord.

*Although I have not seen the future, I know who you are, God. Over my life and throughout the recorded Scriptures, you have proven to me that you are loving, faithful, and true. For this reason, I do not fear the future. I know it is you who holds me and leads me forward.*

# GENUINE LOVE

*Let love be genuine.*
*Abhor what is evil;*
*hold fast to what is good.*
ROMANS 12:9 ESV

Sin can look attractive. The world paints a pretty picture, but it is just a cover-up. The wall underneath the paint is moldy and ugly. The loneliness and emptiness are real. But God's love, on the other hand, is also very real. It is beautiful, and it satisfies the soul. Anything in opposition to God and his ways is evil. We're to abhor what is evil. If we really understood the bigger picture and could see sin for what it is instead of its appearance, then we would abhor it.

Let love be genuine. Real love is neither self-seeking nor misleading. Love is true and good and giving. The world cares about itself and teaches us to do the same. It strokes our egos, promises us pleasure, and turns us away from God. It is truly abhorrent! Choose love. Choose the love that remains forever, is genuine, and is pure.

*God of Love, perhaps I can fool other people with my paint job and the image I wear. I may even fool myself sometimes, but I will never fool you, Father. You know my deepest feelings and fears, and you know love better than anyone, because you are love. Fill me with your genuine love, Lord, and teach me to abhor evil.*

# CARING CORRECTION

*A wise warning to someone who will listen
is as valuable as gold earrings or fine gold jewelry.*
PROVERBS 25:12 NCV

Correcting someone properly can be extremely difficult. First, we can't anticipate how someone else will respond to correction. Second, our own feelings can affect our judgment or the delivery of what we communicate.

The Bible encourages us to speak truth to those who are straying from God. We are not to stay out of it, but to lovingly advise our stumbling brothers and sisters so that they may be saved. We were made to help each other up when we fall. We also must be willing to receive criticism for our behavior. Our bad habits are more apparent to those around us than to ourselves, so listening to the concerns of a trusted friend can bless our spiritual lives.

*God, I ask that you humble my heart. I want to be ready to receive criticism when it comes and to give it if the need arises. Please, teach me to put the spiritual health of others before my feelings of awkwardness or inadequacy.*

# BETTER THAN LIFE

*Because Your favor is better than life,*
*My lips will praise You.*
PSALM 63:3 NASB

Love is the center of the Bible. It would be impossible to consider our religion without it. Why did God send his Son? For the sake of love. Why should we treat people kindly? Because of the love shown to us from our Father. This perfect, steadfast love of God brings praise to the lips of the psalmist. He says God's steady love is better than life, which puts it above the entire realm of human experience.

The psalmist's heart pours forth praise for the one and only God whose love is real, whose love is genuine, and whose love passes the limits of our imagination. May we sing our praise with the emotion of the psalmist. Just as God's love is unfathomable, there will be a day when our worship never ends and our hearts never cease to marvel at the glory of our Savior, Jesus Christ.

*How deep and steadfast is your love, oh Lord. No matter what passes away, you stay the same. Help me to see you clearly today, so that I may be genuine in my devotion and reverence.*

# GODLY GRIEF

*Godly grief produces a repentance that leads to salvation and brings no regret, but worldly grief produces death.*

2 CORINTHIANS 7:10 NRSV

There is a vast difference between godly grief and worldly grief. Godly grief brings conviction and leads to repentance. Worldly grief leads to further sin and destruction. Godly grief leads people to change, humbling themselves enough to go to God to ask for his help and forgiveness. Without God, a person struggling with grief has no option but to suffer through on their own strength. They may try to cover things up with denial, humor, justification, or using something to numb the pain, like drinking too much alcohol or abusing media. Whatever the case, it will lead to more sin and distance from God.

The best way to handle grief is to bring it to God. Whether it was caused by our own actions or something that happened to us, he is ready and able to help us overcome. He offers us the healing, forgiveness, and peace that we need. He can set us on a better path and walk with us. It is never easy to walk through grief, but it is better to walk through it with God than by ourselves.

*Mighty Comforter, please be with me in my grief. Lead me to repentance and walk with me toward healing.*

# EVERY OBSTRUCTION REMOVED

*"Build up, build up, prepare the road!*
*Remove the obstacles out of the way of my people."*
ISAIAH 57:14 NIV

Isaiah's words were directed to the contrite in heart. His words were words of encouragement, meant to breathe new life into the discouraged and distraught. He declared that obstacles be removed from the path. Are there obstacles between you and the Lord? Is there something keeping you from drawing near in prayer to Jesus Christ? Let it be removed. By the power of God, we can remove it, as Isaiah encouraged us to do.

Isaiah said, "Build up, build up, prepare the road." He was saying, on behalf of the Lord, that we should make a way toward our God. We should make a way not just for ourselves, but also those around us. We should not be passive about religion, but active in searching for ways to become closer to and more like Christ.

*Lord, only you can give me the strength to remove the obstacles in my way, so let nothing keep me from running to you. Help me to see how I can point others toward you. Today, may I clear that path to you, my God.*

# TITLE

*He has told you, O man, what is good;*
*and what does the Lord require of you but to do justice,*
*and to love kindness, and to walk humbly with your God?*
MICAH 6:8 ESV

The world is filled with injustices and cruelty, exploitation of the vulnerable, and celebration of evil practices. It hurts God's heart to see the way his children behave. His instructions are clear: we are to practice justice, not harbor prejudices or unfair bias. We are to love kindness, not condone malice. The way we live should reflect a humble walk with God, not a self-indulging mission to advance our own interests.

Regardless of what everyone else is doing, we should deal fairly with everyone. We should love mercy, extend kindness to those around us, and stay humble. This is what the Lord himself demonstrates and what he requires of every believer.

*Dear Lord, I am grateful for the mercy you extend to me. You hate injustice and cruelty. Please, help me be an agent of justice, compassion, and kindness in the world to bring glory to your name.*

# REAL REST

*"Come to me, all who labor and are heavy laden,
and I will give you rest."*
MATTHEW 11:28 ESV

The world we live in preaches business like it's synonymous with success. The appropriate response to "how is your week going?" has to be "busy." Otherwise, we feel like we're not doing as much as we should. Our society has a million and one ways to cope with the stress of our busy lives: mindfulness, meditation, and yoga, to name a few. These things are not inherently bad, but they mean nothing without God's presence. His Word tells us that true rest can only come from him.

When we fix our eyes on Jesus and the end goal, the things of this world start to feel a little less important, and our priorities realign. We are not going to find relief on our phones, in a new business venture, or through a morning coffee ritual. Time spent in God's presence should be at the top of our to-do list every day, or worldly concerns will take up more space in our hearts than the light of Jesus.

*God, thank you for your offer of rest for my weary soul. I get so distracted by the world and its problems that I forget to ground myself in your truth. Help me look to you for my much-needed peace.*

# SOBER-MINDED

*The end of all things is at hand;*
*therefore be self-controlled and sober-minded*
*for the sake of your prayers.*
1 PETER 4:7 ESV

We cannot get distracted by temporal problems if we want to pray over what is important. Our life is short, and the possibility not leaving an impact is high. This reality stands behind Peter's words, "be self-controlled and sober-minded." Our prayers must keep Christ at the forefront of our minds by loving, thinking, and acting in his name.

The greatest tragedy is not to live a life of pain but one of apathy or self-indulgence. The person whose life is a wreck knows that they have lost something, but the person drowning in pleasure is fooled into thinking that they have gained the world. This is why suffering is seen as a blessing to Christians. Suffering inspires prayer. Peter reminds us that we should not need suffering to be sober-minded. Think about the impending end of everything around us and the desperate importance of what we do, and then pray.

*Oh God, there is so much good I can do in the life you have granted me. Give me eyes to see the importance of my actions and choices. Give me the strength to remain focused on the things of heaven and not my fleeting life.*

# IRON SHARPENS IRON

*As iron sharpens iron,*
*so a friend sharpens a friend.*
PROVERBS 27:17 NLT

Iron does not sharpen easily. When this proverb was penned, sharpening iron took a lot of time, skill, and work. It required detail and awareness. Like sharpening iron, relationships are not easily sharpened or maintained; they take work, awareness, and invested time. To reach the point in a friendship where two people can point out each other's flaws and help smooth them out requires a level of trust which can only be forged carefully over time.

We were fashioned for family and friends. That is the way our Lord intended it. In this broken world are many broken relationships, but we are not supposed to walk alone. A good friend is worth the work of sharpening the friendship. We are here to help others, and the Lord knows we also need the help of others.

*Father, thank you for never giving up on me, instead carefully sharpening and refining me. Please put people in my life who are not afraid to help me smooth out my rough patches.*

# STEP OF FAITH

*He said, "Come." And when Peter had come down out of the boat,*
*he walked on the water to go to Jesus.*
MATTHEW 14:29 NKJV

Jesus called us to come. He did not say it would be easy. The road is riddled with difficulties. He may call someone to give their money to the poor, someone else to move to the farthest corner of the world, or another to be faithful in their daily grind at home. He may lead us to serve a family or to find contentment with him in our singleness.

Are you lacking a purpose, feeling overwhelmed by your workload, or simply missing connection with God? Take a step of faith. Climb out of the boat and trust him. Even if you start to sink, and we all will from time to time, he is right beside you, ready to catch you. On whatever road he leads you, take his hand and trust him.

*Jesus, only in you can I find the path to life. No matter what you have called me to do, I will take your hand and trust in you. Thank you for never letting me go.*

# THE LORD DELIVERS

*The righteous person may have many troubles,*
*but the LORD delivers him from them all.*
PSALM 34:19 NIV

Both the righteous and the unrighteous will face troubling times, and the Lord is faithful to deliver them both if they would only turn to him and obey. Matthew 5:45 says, "He causes his sun to rise on the evil and the good, and sends rain on the righteous and the unrighteous." In this life, we are guaranteed to have problems, but the difference between us and the unrighteous is that the Lord will deliver us and flood us with his peace.

The Lord is in charge of the world and of us. He is the King and Creator of all. He guides the sun and sends the rain, and he is more than willing to guide us through the snares and into his abundance. Rather than turning to unrighteous navigation options, run to the one who is over all and in all. He has the answers for every situation and occasion.

*Thank you for your deliverance, Almighty God! As I pursue you, I become more righteous, and I find hope in times of trouble. You supply me with answers for every daunting question. Please, lead me home.*

# ON GOD'S SIDE

*What should we say about this?*
*If God is for us, no one can defeat us.*
ROMANS 8:31 NCV

No one and nothing can stand in opposition to our heavenly Creator. There is no power in existence superior to our Father. No force can move us away from the Holy One who sustains us and holds us with his mighty hand. Although the world's winds may howl and the enemy throws his threats around, we are rooted in Christ. Nothing can break us down. We can trust God when he promises to keep us safe, for he has never broken a promise, and he never will.

Our Lord and Savior did not even withhold his own life from us, so why would he withhold his protection now? Not even death could defeat him. Our hope in him is certain because his character is proven and good. We are on God's side, and no one can defeat us.

*Who do I have to fear but you, Lord God? Who would dare to oppose the Almighty? I trust you completely and turn to you for security. Nothing else can offer me the life that you provide.*

# GOD'S INFLUENCE

*Instead, you ought to say, "If the Lord wills,*
*we will live and also do this or that."*

JAMES 4:15 NCV

Our world makes it easy to forget that God participates in the events of our lives. We begin to think that enough planning and execution can help us achieve anything. Then something happens, and our lives are turned upside down. This was the situation of James' audience. They had begun to forget God's counsel and not recognize his influence in their lives.

They were wrong, though. Not only does God affect how our daily lives play out, but we also depend on him for every positive circumstance. Job promotions, healthy children, and sound relationships are all from God. Recognizing this gives us a new perspective from which we can say, "If the Lord wills, we will live and do this or that."

*You are working in my life, Lord. Nothing happens outside of your observation or influence. Thank you, God, for all the blessings in my life. I recognize them today, and they inspire me to recognize you in my plans and endeavors.*

# HE GIVES GRACE

*He gives more grace. Therefore it says,*
*"God opposes the proud, but gives grace to the humble."*

JAMES 4:6 ESV

The point of James' message addressed the quarreling which was becoming more common among the early believers. They were falling into the snare of pursuing their own personal agendas and successes rather than caring for one another, as is expected within the body of Christ. James warned them that God stood in opposition of their proud pursuits. The work of the cross is to care for one another; that was the message Jesus came to demonstrate.

These believers had lost sight of the grace they were supposed to be emulating, and they were chasing their own glories instead. This is a reminder to us to stay humble. God gives grace to those who are humble before him, and pride will only get in the way.

*Father, I am sorry the times when my arrogance gets in the way and I selfishly seek attention and glory for myself. I ask humbly for your grace. Help me redirect my heart back to you as I look out for the needs of others. I will rejoice when it is their turn for recognition or praise. Forgive me, dear Father.*

# NOVEMBER

Serving God does make us very rich,
if we are satisfied with what we have.
We brought nothing into the world,
so we can take nothing out.
But, if we have food and clothes,
we will be satisfied with that.

1 TIMOTHY 6:6-8 NCV

# CONFIDENCE IN HOPE

*"You will have confidence, because there is hope;
you will be protected and take your rest in safety."*
JOB 11:18 NRSV

Those of us who depend on God have no need to fear the future. Regardless of what we read or see on the news, our God is the same as he always has been, and he has our best in mind. We have confidence because we know our hope is wisely placed in him who cannot be moved or overthrown. Every day is in God's hands, the same God who created the world and imagined the stars, who taught waterfalls how to flow and birds how to fly.

Whenever we feel afraid, we can read God's Word and find reminders of how he cares for his children. Matthew 10:28 puts this in perspective for us. "Do not fear those who kill the body but cannot kill the soul; rather fear him who can destroy both soul and body in hell." Job experienced this firsthand, and he kept his confidence in the Lord.

*God my Maker, teach me, through your servant Job and through your limitless other examples, that I can have full confidence in you. In you I place my hope, and I rest peacefully knowing that you're in control of my life.*

# RIGHTEOUS PRAYERS

*Confess your sins to each other and pray for each other so that you may be healed. The earnest prayer of a righteous person has great power and produces wonderful results.*

JAMES 5:16 NLT

It is never easy to confess our sins. When we have people around us who we have invited into our lives, who we know will stand by us in tough times, it is a lot easier. We should admit our sins to our brothers and sisters, so that they can pray for us and help us through.

By praying, checking in, and helping to find answers or alternatives, it becomes evident yet again that the body works best together with all its members. We need the prayers of others. We were made to need each other. A righteous person who prays sincerely will surely see incredible results from the Lord. We want to be these people, and we want to know these people. There is great power in righteous, earnest prayers.

*Dear God, please forgive me for my sins. Surround me with people who are willing to listen lovingly and to pray for me. Show me who needs my prayers and who I can encourage today.*

# GOD HEARD ME

*Certainly God has heard me;*
*He has attended to the voice of my prayer.*

PSALM 66:19 NKJV

If you've ever felt lost in a crowd, alone in your thoughts, or misunderstood, then you know how powerful it is when someone listens and truly hears you. We all want to be heard and understood. Praying may sometimes seem one-sided, but it isn't. God hears every word we whisper and even the ones we don't.

Our Maker loves us completely and truly hears us. We are not drowned out by grander prayers elsewhere; he leans in and listens to every cry of our hearts because he cares deeply about his children. He attends to us. We may not always see the results, but he is with us, attending to us constantly, as our loving Father.

*Thank you for listening, Father God, and for truly hearing me. Thank you for understanding me and attending to all my needs. I praise you for your love, care, and grace. In moments when I feel alone or misunderstood, remind me that I serve a God who perfectly contradicts these lies.*

# FELLOWSHIP

*The Lord God said,*
*"It is not good for the man to be alone.*
*I will make a helper suitable for him."*
GENESIS 2:18 NIV

Being part of a community can be intimidating. Whatever picture it evokes in our heads can be something that makes us uncomfortable. We may think we don't need to engage with other believers, but God saw from the beginning that humans are not suited to isolation. He gave Adam all the animals of the world, but it wasn't enough; he needed another person. God wants his people to engage in each other's lives, to rejoice and laugh with each other, to rest and to work together.

Spending time with fellow Christians brings encouragement, insight, and knowledge in a way we can't achieve by ourselves. Talking with others can help us see things about God, the world, and our own behavior that we might miss. God's intent for community is that we build each other up and strengthen each other, so that we are better equipped to share his Word.

*God, help me to remember that I need other people. I like to be by myself, and spending time with other believers can feel like a chore. Help me to see the amazing ways you use my fellowship with others for the good of your kingdom.*

# WHAT YOU WANT

*"Do to others what you want them to do to you.*
*This is the meaning of the law of Moses*
*and the teaching of the prophets."*
MATTHEW 7:12 NCV

There is an infinite amount of ways we can offend God and turn our backs on him. Reading about the Old Testament law, we see how many ceremonies it took just to be symbolically clean, let alone actually pure. Through the prophets, we see our own stories of rebellion mirrored by the people of Israel, who turned their backs on God time and time again.

The ways we have fallen short of glory, the ways we dishonor God, are too many to count. It is impossible for anyone to avoid committing them. Yet there is one way to glorify God. By trusting in Christ, we are made righteous. In this righteousness, we learn to desire what is truly good, and so we become aware of what we want others to do for us, and better yet, how we can do the same for them. Christ reveals to us what it means for a person to flourish, alive and joyful, and this guides us to treat others.

*Dear Lord, may I do for others what I would like for myself. May I bless them in the ways you have blessed me. Only you can reveal what those around me need, so please show me clearly. By your strength, may I be a blessing for my brothers and sisters.*

# UNITY IN LOVE

*In addition to all these things put on love,*
*which is the perfect bond of unity.*
COLOSSIANS 3:14 NASB

God wants his people to live together as members of the same body. If the body of Christ is divided, it won't thrive. We cannot expect to have grudges or divisions without repercussions; our spiritual well-being will suffer.

How do we not separate ourselves from others? Paul tells us that love is "the perfect bond of unity." We must bear with one another and forgive each other, showing genuine love that is not dictated by passing emotion or fading loyalty. More than just showing love, though, we must put on love, as if it were a garment or uniform that people can identify. We must love as Christ loved, to the very end.

*Lord, I should base my love for others on your love for me. Teach me to show this supernatural love in my speech, actions, and decisions. Help me rise above the easy hatred and fury that the world offers every day.*

# HE CAME FOR SINNERS

*"I have not come to call the righteous
but sinners to repentance."*
LUKE 5:32 ESV

Although we deserved death and judgment, the Lord Jesus came to offer us life and forgiveness. The key point of this verse is that we are all sinners. Not one of us is righteous on our own. In fact, Romans 3:10 says that "None is righteous, no, not one." Christ came for the sinners, but we are all sinners. Those who believe themselves to be righteous are still sinners in need of salvation, but they cannot be helped because they do not recognize their need for Jesus' help.

We who realize that we are sinners in need of Christ's forgiveness are grateful for his grace and accepting of his forgiveness and help. He is not calling those who think they can do it on their own; he is calling those who know they cannot.

*I am desperate for your help, Lord Jesus. I am utterly hopeless without you. Thank you for coming to me and calling me to you. Thank you for not rejecting me because of my sin. Instead you took my disgusting sin upon yourself and freed me forever. Alleluia!*

# LAYING DOWN OUR LIVES

*We know love by this, that he laid down his life for us—*
*and we ought to lay down our lives for one another.*
1 JOHN 3:16 NRSV

By laying his life down, Christ forever instituted love as a sacrificial practice. As John says, we know love by the example Christ set us in laying down his life for us. Perfect in glory and righteousness, he counted his life—his precious, beautiful life—something not worth holding onto. He counted our safety worth more than his own, and even gave up his bond to the Father briefly so we might be saved. What are we willing to sacrifice for one another?

Christ is above all. We may never be asked to lay down our lives for someone, but whenever we must give something up for the sake of others, we can look to what Christ did. He withheld nothing. Is there anything that we are unwilling to give up?

*Oh, precious Lord Jesus, how much you have given to redeem me. Help me to show love just as you loved me in giving up your life. Even if it takes my own life, may I never withhold anything from another out of selfishness.*

# DON'T WORRY

*"Don't be concerned about what to eat and what to drink.*
*Don't worry about such things."*
LUKE 12:29 NLT

Much of our lives is consumed with meal planning, grocery shopping, cooking, and cleaning. At times, money might be tight, or budgeting difficult. It is wise to learn how to live within our means plan accordingly, but it gets the better of us is when we begin to worry about the future unnecessarily. It is unnecessary because the Lord has always been and always will be faithful to his followers.

Of course, Christians still suffer and go without. Some even starve! No matter what happens or what we endure in this life, the Lord assures us that we needn't worry. He has far better things in store for us than this world. Our physical needs demand our attention, but they should not command our hearts.

*You teach me not to worry, dear Jesus, and you prove your love and loyalty to me over and over. Yet my heart is quick to wander and doubt. Please, remind me to set my mind on the things that matter, and to not become distraught over temporary concerns.*

# BE STRONG

*Remember to stay alert and hold firmly to all that you believe.*
*Be mighty and full of courage.*
1 CORINTHIANS 16:13 TPT

Fear and weakness are conquered by this verse. It is the voice of God urging us toward strength and wisdom. Paul tells us to be watchful, lest we fall into willful ignorance and abandon our intelligence and alertness. He tells us to stand firm because doubts will try to erode our foundation of faith. In our watchfulness and firmness, we are reminded to be strong, which is natural when our God is almighty and dedicated to our redemption.

We have an unchanging God of might worth trusting in. He is not aloof or unpredictable. If there was a possibility of God forsaking us, we would have no reason to be firm in our faith. Our every waking and sleeping effort would be aimed at securing Christ's favor. Thank God that we have a promised salvation! We are secure in our relationship with him, which inspires strength in us.

*Gracious Lord Jesus, keep me watchful. Remind me of the promised inheritance I have on high. Remind me that I am strong in you. Thank you for giving me faith and strength beyond my ability.*

# BLESSINGS

*"Because of your father's God, who helps you, because of the Almighty, who blesses you with blessings of the skies above, blessings of the deep springs below, blessings of the breast and womb."*
GENESIS 49:25 NIV

Our God is recognizable. We might be amazed at how we arrived where we are. We can look back at the years behind us, the crucial decisions that we did or didn't mess up, and we can wonder how God managed to lead us to where we are. The answer to this question is the same answer Jacob gave his sons: "Because of your father's God, who helps you."

If we would only turn our eyes to the blessings in our life, to the "blessings of the sky above, blessings of the deep springs below," we would see how powerful God is. This is the same God who directs our life and holds us in his hand. Why do we fear for our future when he is on our side?

*Oh God, my heavenly Father, you have so richly blessed me. I stand amazed this day at how you lead me, step by step. Let the blessings you have showered on your people be a reminder of your care for me.*

# THE UNCHANGING ONE

*Jesus Christ is the same yesterday
and today, and forever.*
HEBREWS 13:8 NASB

Things in life grow and adapt over time. Cultures take on new customs and lose touch with old ones. Vegetation is plowed down, animals are domesticated, and some go extinct. People are influenced and change over time, whether for good or bad. The only constant is our unchanging God Almighty. He always has been perfectly good and loving, and he always will be. He is the Ancient of Days whose reign is for all eternity. Jesus Christ always has been, and always will be, the one we can trust with our full confidence.

When life throws us curveballs and surprises, we can adapt and embrace them, relying on Christ's unaltered nature to be our anchor and compass. If we root ourselves in his truth, he becomes the focal point of our lives. No matter what, we will be secure.

*Through your truth, I perceive the rest of life, Lord Jesus. Focusing on you as my Savior affects whether I accept or deny other things I am told. Your Word is unwavering, and your nature is pure. Nothing else is certain outside of my relationship with you.*

# WISDOM FROM GOD

*When the people of Israel heard about King Solomon's decision,
they respected him very much. They saw he had wisdom from God
to make the right decisions.*

1 KINGS 3:28 NCV

We can see the Lord working in King Solomon. While many kings would have asked for power or wealth from God, Solomon asked for wisdom, and in return received everything he could have asked for. His decision to honor the Lord naturally blessed him on a spiritual level, but it also brought respect and honor to him from those around him. They could see the extraordinary working of the Holy Spirit in their king.

How does our relationship with God alter others' perceptions of us? Do they look at our lives and marvel at how the Lord is at work in his people? Our natural thought would be to strive toward honoring ourselves, but we should do what Solomon did. Simply desire God and his wisdom.

*Lord, there are so many things I could ask for. I am one of your people, and I entrust my every need to you. Still, it is sometimes hard to remember what is worth praying for. Make wisdom, virtue, and faithfulness my prayer, for they will help me honor you.*

# FORGIVENESS IS WAITING

*Whoever conceals his transgressions will not prosper,
but he who confesses and forsakes them will obtain mercy.*
PROVERBS 28:13 ESV

We often try to hide our mistakes. We want people to see us as we want to be—flawless. God tells us that instead of holding on to the mistakes we make, we should confess them. We will find him waiting with forgiveness. Denying our sins only traps them in our hearts and minds. Asking for forgiveness releases them to God, who is the only one with the power to totally take them away and make us pure again.

Failing, unfortunately, is an unavoidable part of life. Are we going to try to disguise our shortcomings and pretend they don't exist? Or are we going to acknowledge them and learn from them? The Bible says that God's power is made perfect in weakness. When we sin, God can use that moment to teach us and others, showing us the power he has to forgive and to make bad things work for the good of his kingdom. Your mistakes are never too much for God to forgive.

*God, I ask you now for your forgiveness. I have made mistakes and hurt you, as well as the people around me. I want to do better in the future. Please, work through the bad situations I have caused and use them for your goodness and glory.*

# PERFECT IN PATIENCE

*I was given mercy so that in me, the worst of all sinners,*
*Christ Jesus could show that he has patience without limit.*
*His patience with me made me an example for those*
*who would believe in him and have life forever.*

1 TIMOTHY 1:16 NCV

There is no limit to God's patience. No sin, no rebellion, no hatred can turn God away from his plan to save us. If something could, God would not be all-powerful. Even Paul, who had made it his life's purpose to persecute the early church, was saved by God, showing just how far his kindness can reach. Paul was the benefactor of Christ's perfect patience.

May all those around us witness the lengths Christ will go to save a single sinner. Paul received mercy even though he was a willful sinner. He was redeemed and made into one of the primary figures of the New Testament. There is no limit to what God is willing to do to save your soul. If he has decided that you will be his child, it is only a matter of time.

*Lord, there is nothing you will stop at to redeem a sinner's heart. Remind me of your persistence today. May I be just as determined in reaching the poor of this world.*

# GOOD GOD

*"Why do you call me good?" Jesus asked.*
*"Only God is truly good."*
MARK 10:18 NLT

Jesus wanted the ruler, who had called Jesus good, to consider the words he was speaking. Of course, Jesus knew he was everything that was good. But did the ruler understand what he was saying? "Why do you call me good?" Jesus asked him. Had the ruler considered what made him good, or who he truly was? Jesus had demonstrated his goodness, and there was no doubt that Jesus was in fact good. But why? How?

"Only God is truly good," Jesus pointed out. He was encouraging the ruler to conclude by his own confession what he must have known in his heart to be true; Jesus Christ is God himself. His actions proved it, his miracles confirmed it, and that truth resonates in the hearts of every person, whether they are ready to admit it or not.

*Give me clarity and wisdom, Christ Jesus. I know who you are, and I want to worship you. Rather than come to earth to demand obedience, you demonstrated your character to us. There is nothing left to conclude but that you are the Most High himself, fully good and fully God.*

# A TRUE FRIEND

*One who has unreliable friends soon comes to ruin,*
*but there is a friend who sticks closer than a brother.*
PROVERBS 18:24 NIV

God has brought other believers into our lives so that we can keep each other accountable, encourage one another, offer help in times of trouble, and celebrate the good times. It's easy to see that those we spend the most time with will have the most influence on our lives. A friend who has proven to be unreliable and dishonest should not influence our lives or be the one we turn to. We can still love and care about such people, but if we are going to them for help, we will find ourselves in ruin.

A true, reliable friend is someone who will offer us good advice, even if it's not what we want to hear. They will stick with us through difficult times, and they can be even closer than family. When we find a friend like this, we should invest in this friendship and keep it close.

*Lord, thank you for being my best friend. Thank you also for putting people in my life who can help me. Please, give me wisdom to identify such friends and to be that kind of friend to others.*

# RESPECT AND FEAR

*Let us be thankful, because we have a kingdom that cannot be shaken.*
*We should worship God in a way that pleases him with respect and fear.*
HEBREWS 12:28 NCV

How much of our prayers are worship and adoration of our Holy God? He has already given us more than we can comprehend. Bringing our requests and fears to the Lord is not wrong; in fact, he urges us to. But if the only time we go to the Lord is in supplication, then our relationship with him is only as deep as our perceived need.

The Mighty One, the Maker of heaven and earth, love and life, is worthy of our praise and thanksgiving. In fact, it is an honor and a privilege to worship him for who he is, in addition to what he has done. Praising God for his wonderful works and perfect character not only gives him the reverence he deserves; it reminds our hearts of who the God we serve truly is. It fills our hearts and encourages our faith. When we give to God purely out of the gratitude of our hearts, he finds a way to give right back to us.

*With all the respect and fear I possess, I praise your name, Father God! I worship you for who you are. Thank you for all you've done.*

# CONFIDENT PRAYER

*The prayer of faith will save the sick, and the Lord will raise him up.*
*And if he has committed sins, he will be forgiven.*

JAMES 5:15 NKJV

God has a plan for our prayer lives. Yes, he already knows what will happen in the future, but he has also planned for our prayers to instigate events that are to come. The Bible tells us that the prayer of a righteous person has great power. That means believers who have been made righteous by Jesus' sacrifice have the power to speak healing and light into people's lives, if it is God's will.

The only way to know God's will is to read his Word consistently and talk with him. We don't get to know our best friend by monologuing and telling them everything we want. We listen as well, wait patiently for them to share with us, and ask questions to understand them better.

*Father, I ramble to you far too often, and I forget that you have something to say to me, too. Open my heart to hear you, that I may know your will and use that knowledge to help your people.*

# WHATEVER YOU DO

*Let every activity of your lives and every word that comes from your lips be drenched with the beauty of our Lord Jesus, the Anointed One. And bring your constant praise to God the Father because of what Christ has done for you!*

COLOSSIANS 3:17 TPT

The Father and Son are both present in our actions. In this passage, Paul is teaching us how we behave more as Christ did and how we become more transformed into his image. It does not end there, though. We do this for the reputation and glory of God the Father, living in thankfulness to him.

This passage is much more than an exhortation to act like a Christian. It describes the transformation at work in a believer. After Jesus Christ opens the path for us to enter into regular fellowship with God, the Holy Spirit begins to shape us though our actions, so that we can live with hearts that praise and glorify God the Father. "Whatever we do, in word or deed," is more than just habits and routines. It is God, slowing transforming us into his image.

*I offer up my actions to you, God. Make me into the child of God that I was made to be. I yield my silent, unconscious habits to you, so that you may use them to shape me. Thank you, God, for making change possible in the hearts of once-lost sinners and hypocrites.*

# SPIRIT OF THE LORD

*The Spirit of the Lord will rest on Him,*
*The spirit of wisdom and understanding,*
*The spirit of counsel and strength,*
*The spirit of knowledge and the fear of the Lord.*
ISAIAH 11:2 NASB

There should have been no mistaking Jesus when he appeared to mankind. The prophets of old all testified of his coming, and when he opened his mouth, the truths of God poured out. It was evident to all with faith that the Spirit of God rested on him.

In everything he did or said, he had the wisdom of God and a heavenly understanding. He gave divine counsel and showed supernatural strength. He lived with the fear of the Lord present in his decisions. He had knowledge of the heavenly realm that couldn't exist outside of God. Before ascending back to heaven after his resurrection, he promised to leave that same Spirit with us to lead us, counsel us, and teach us the wisdom of God.

*Your wisdom and understanding fill me, Lord. Your Spirit is all I need for counsel, strength, and knowledge of you. I will choose to listen and obey.*

# PRESERVATION

*"You gave me life and showed me kindness,*
*and in your providence watched over my spirit."*
JOB 10:12 NIV

Why are we still alive? Think back on the times when your life could have ended. If you can't think of any, even getting into a car is a risk. The only reason you survived anything, no matter how slightly dangerous, is because of God's care for you. In those moments of possible detriment, God decided to preserve your life. He has granted us life and steadfast love, and he protected us from danger.

The care God has for our spirit is one of the most tender ways he manifests his love for us. Not one person the Father has entrusted to the Son has been forgotten or forsaken, because God is perfect in preserving us. He is the ultimate object of our trust, one which will never fail us.

*God, to you I entrust my life. To you I give thanks for my life, which has been preserved for now on earth and will be preserved forever in heaven. Today, I pray for your steadfast love to work in me and be evident to all who see me.*

# WASHING FEET

*He poured water into the basin, and began washing the disciples' feet
and wiping them with the towel which He had tied around Himself.*
JOHN 13:5 NASB

The washing of feet in Jewish culture was something only done
by servants for their masters. It was unheard of, and looked down
upon, for someone to disgrace themselves by washing another
person's feet. Yet as Jesus often did, he flipped this notion on its
head and washed his disciples' feet.

Jesus is King of the universe, yet he was willing to kneel on the
floor and wash the feet of his flawed human servants. He did this to
communicate two things. First, he was not looking for those who
would only obediently serve him. He wanted loving friends who
would lay down their lives for him, the same way he was about to
for them. Second, he did this to give us an example of what true
leadership and love looks like in action. He does not care who
has the most riches, and neither should we. The currency of his
kingdom is love.

*Oh Jesus, you are the greatest, and yet you became the
least of all, thus redefining greatness. Teach me to be more
like you.*

# THE TORN VEIL

*Let us therefore approach the throne of grace with boldness,*
*so that we may receive mercy and find grace to help in time of need.*
HEBREWS 4:16 NRSV

In the Old Testament, we learn about a place called the Holy of Holies. It was the innermost part of the Israelites' place of worship, separated by a heavy veil, where God's presence would appear once a year to the high priest on the day of atonement. This separation told the Israelites that there was a distinct gap between God's holiness and their sinful humanity. God was inaccessible to the people, even though he guided them and loved them.

When Jesus cried out as he died on the cross, that veil was torn from top to bottom, signifying that the barrier between us and God was broken. Our sin was atoned for, once and for all. We can now come before God in prayer with the assurance that our guilt has been taken away forever.

*Lord God, I know that your sacrifice to redeem me*
*was costly. Thank you for not holding back your only Son,*
*through whom we are rescued. You are so full of love for*
*your people, and I praise you for giving me the gift of*
*freedom and access to your kingdom.*

# REDEMPTION

*Create in me a clean heart, O God,*
*and put a new and right spirit within me.*
PSALM 51:10 NRSV

Our sinful way of living is an abomination in Jesus Christ's sight. He is pure and righteous, so he understands the absolute evil of our careless sins and mistakes. Even among Christians, any human failing that is not taboo is laughed over and shrugged off. God does not shrug off our sin. It pains him, raising mountains of indignation in his heart, for he sent his Son to suffer torture and die to give us purity.

Is there any doubt why David is crying out to God for forgiveness? He sees the depths of his sin, how intolerable it is to our Lord and Savior, and he sees that God did nothing to incite it in us. There is no excuse for our moral imperfection. Hoping for a right spirit to be renewed in him, David prays earnestly to God for restoration. May we yearn just as earnestly as he did for righteousness and purity.

*Lord, you are able to make me right with you. You can create in me a new, clean heart. Please, forgive me for my sins. Restore me from all the ways I have rebelled against you. I hope in your salvation this day.*

# BELIEVE IN JESUS

*"Will you never believe in me unless you see
miraculous signs and wonders?"*

JOHN 4:48 NLT

As wonderful as it is to be amazed at Christ's miracles and to witness his wonders, they are not what faith is based on. Anyone who truly desires God and wants to know him personally will read his Word and take it to heart. Those who do will discover that the entire thing, from cover to cover, was written about Jesus Christ and his divinity. The Old Testament is a constant foreshadowing of the Messiah, and the New Testament is a testimony of his life.

If we cannot read and recognize that the only possible, honest conclusion we can draw is that Jesus Christ is God himself, then no number of miraculous signs and wonders will convince us, either. We either believe Jesus is who he said he is, or we don't. We are either ready to accept the truth laid out in the Scriptures, or we are not.

*Messiah, when you send your signs and wonders, I am grateful. But when you don't, I will worship you just the same. You do not owe me proof, yet you offer it willingly. I believe in you, Christ Jesus!*

# PEACE OF GOD

*All this is from God. Through Christ, God made peace between us*
*and himself, and God gave us the work of telling everyone*
*the peace we can have with him.*

2 CORINTHIANS 5:18 NCV

The peace of God is a remarkable thing. When Adam and Eve
sinned, they formed enmity between us and God and hostility
between us and creation. However, God came down and restored
the relationship between humanity and himself. He established an
everlasting peace that comes only through knowing and accepting
Christ as Lord of our lives.

As reestablished children of the Most High, our commission is
to tell others of this peace we have in Christ. God made peace
between us and himself, but so many are not living in this peace. It
could be theirs, but they need someone to show them the way.

*Almighty Lord, thank you for reconciling me to yourself*
*through Christ Jesus. I am forever grateful for your sacrifice,*
*which restored me to you. Be exalted and magnified through*
*me, Lord, and may I live a life worthy of your calling.*

# DILIGENCE

*Diligent hands will rule,*
*but laziness ends in forced labor.*
PROVERBS 12:24 NIV

There is a divine quality woven into work that comes straight from God himself. Doing good, honest work is part of worshipping and glorifying God. When we work with pure intentions and a grateful attitude, it is fulfilling because it gives us purpose and direction, but also because it brings honor to God.

When we engage in work, both spiritual and physical, we are fulfilling the mandate of God gave to his creation. Even he worked for six days to create the world before resting the seventh day. He set a precedent as our Father and Maker for us to follow, and we ought to diligently seek to do so.

*Creator God, you made me in your image and gave me the ability to work and be creative. This is who you are, and who you fashioned me to be. I want to be diligent and consistent in all that I do, in all work I've been allotted and in the mandates you have given. I want to be like you, dear Father.*

# PERSEVERANCE

*You need to persevere so that when you have done the will of God,*
*you will receive what he has promised.*
HEBREWS 10:36 NIV

Maintaining a walk of faith is not an easy journey. It can be overwhelming and daunting when everything seems to go against the biblical principles we cling to. Paul urged the church to persevere and stay strong through hardships, because he knew it was not in vain to follow God and stand in opposition to evil. In the end, we shall overcome if we keep faith. Those who persevere and do not lose sight of grace will be triumphant when God's name is exalted throughout the earth.

Remember that we are never alone in our walk of faith. The Holy Spirit guides us and gives us strength to keep going. We find peace in God's Word. We are also encouraged by fellow sisters and brothers who are on their own walk of faith. Together, we move toward the finish line. In the end, we will receive God's promises.

*Lord, the path you have me on becomes so tough at times. I ask for strength and perseverance to make it to the end and receive your prize through Christ Jesus.*

# THE FATHER'S LOVE

*Don't set the affections of your heart on this world or in loving the things of the world. The love of the Father and the love of the world are incompatible.*

1 JOHN 2:15 TPT

What occupies our hearts? What do we treasure? If the answer to these questions leads our minds away from God, then we should look closely at John's commandment. The world around us offers itself as an object of our adoration. We are drawn in by a sense of wonder or desire, but it is not true wonder or desire. Created things could never incite in us the same response the Creator does. That is why John does not want us to love the world or the things in it.

If the world were worthy of our love, there would be no sin in loving it. We are allowed to admire the beauty of God's creation, but the person who created all things is the only one worthy of adoration. Only the Lord Jesus Christ is worthy to be praised, and only he can live up to our expectations of a Savior. If anyone adores the things God created above the God who created them, the true love of God is not in them.

*Lord, raise up in me a love for what is right. Every day, help me to see how you are worthy of all praise, and with this thought may I love you.*

# DECEMBER

All Scripture is inspired by God and is useful
to teach us what is true and to make us
realize what is wrong in our lives. It corrects us
when we are wrong and teaches us to
do what is right. God uses it to prepare and
equip his people to do every good work.

2 TIMOTHY 3:16-17 NLT

# WISDOM AND UNDERSTANDING

*Blessed is a person who finds wisdom,*
*And one who obtains understanding.*

PROVERBS 3:13 NASB

Where is wisdom found? God told Job that "the fear of the Lord, that is wisdom; and to turn away from evil is understanding" (Job 28:28). King Solomon knew the value of wisdom and understanding when he wrote this proverb. He realized that our lives are far more blessed when we understand the things God wants to reveal to us. Therefore, our lives will be far more blessed when we reverently fear the Lord and turn away from evil.

Although some evil ways may seem pleasing at the time, they offer no lasting benefit or blessing. It is to God's glory and our advantage that we listen to his Word and heed his ways. He gave us perfect instructions because he knew they would lead us to the best lives possible.

*Knowing you brings clarity to every part of my life, Lord God. Through you and through abiding to your ways, I grow in true wisdom and understanding, which in turn blesses me immensely. Thank you!*

# THE COMING GLORY

*We all, with unveiled face, beholding as in a mirror the glory of the Lord, are being transformed into the same image from glory to glory, just as by the Spirit of the Lord.*

2 CORINTHIANS 3:18 NKJV

We are image-bearers. While the rest of the world, like a broken mirror, reflects the nature of our intelligent Creator, we bear his character. We are his children, being "transformed into the same image from glory to glory." If the people in our world are to know what their Savior looks like, we must be the reflections of his grace that point them in the right direction.

How do we begin to resemble our Father? The apostle Paul says it comes about "with unveiled face, beholding as in a mirror the glory of the Lord." We are transformed into the likeness of God just by setting him before our eyes. Transformation does not come from working hard or managing our sins. It just comes from lifting our eyes to God, with unveiled face.

*God, why do I set useless things before my eyes? Be the center of my attention today, as I trust in you for my holy transformation.*

# ETERNAL FOOD

*"Don't work for the food that spoils. Work for the food that stays good always and gives eternal life. The Son of Man will give you this food, because on him God the Father has put his power."*
JOHN 6:27 NCV

Due to our physical nature and the demands of our bodies, it is necessary that we work for food. But what is our motivation? What inspires us to keep our bodies running? With what attitude do we approach this temporary work? Why would we work our lives away for bodies that will someday break down and perish, unless we were eternally motivated?

Eternal food nourishes us now and has eternal benefit. Praying to God and growing our bond with him is eternal. Reading his Word and instilling in ourselves a heavenly mindset is eternal. Loving and serving others who are also dearly loved of God has eternal benefits, because it is what the Lord commanded us to do. While we go about the necessary task of working to fulfill our temporary needs, it should always be for the sake of the gospel: for eternal food that never perishes.

*Please, nourish me with food that never perishes, Father. Fill me with hope, love, grace, and more as I commit my daily work to you with a positive and grateful attitude.*

# OUT OF NOTHING

*It is by faith we understand that the whole world
was made by God's command so what we see
was made by something that cannot be seen.*
HEBREWS 11:3 NCV

As Christians, we believe that God created the universe with
just the power of his word. Everything he made, he made to be
beautiful and to bring him glory. God's power goes beyond our
comprehension. He did not need existing materials to change and
shape into what he wanted; all he had to do was speak the world
into existence, and it was.

God speaks incredible things into being, even when we cannot see
their origin. We may not see the ways God works in our lives, but
God reveals to us just what we need to know at exactly the right
time. God's wisdom is perfect, and we can trust that wisdom. Our
faith is all he asks for in return.

*God, your power is high above my words. I can't even try
to understand it, but I praise you for using it for the good
of those who love you. Sometimes, I struggle to have faith
when I can't see your plan working in my life. Help me to
trust you through the process.*

# GOD'S CONSCIENCE

*Whether you turn to the right or to the left,*
*your ears will hear a voice behind you, saying,*
*"This is the way; walk in it."*
ISAIAH 30:21 NIV

Our conscience is not us deciding to honor God, but rather God telling us how to honor him. He is the voice behind you, the person saying, "This is the way, walk in it." Even the inclination to do what is good doesn't bring us credit!

For the good people who are unredeemed, there is a great warning. God has blessed them greatly with a mind that discerns good from evil, but they still haven't turned to repentance. They have taken God's richest blessing and shown no gratitude to him. We, the children of God, just as much as them, should give thanks to the Lord for the blessing of a conscience.

*Oh God, all things are to your glory. Thank you for showing me the right path, leading me in it, and keeping me on it. Even when I depart from your instruction, you will not abandon me. Your grace is new every day. Praise you, Father!*

# FREEDOM

*As God's loving servants, you should live in complete freedom,*
*but never use your freedom as a cover-up for evil.*
1 PETER 2:16 TPT

Our freedom has been completed by the sacrifice of Christ, but do we truly live in this freedom? How often do we enslave ourselves mentally again, living in guilt or refusing to find help to break free of sin? How closely do we hug the sidelines of sinful living because we know we serve a loving and forgiving God?

God does love us, but if we are truly his devoted and caring children, why would we abuse his love to cover up the evil we partake in? Forgiveness is not granted so that our sin and selfishness may continue. It is there to offer us second, third, and forth chances to get back on track. Our Father is patient with us and quick to forgive, so let's take advantage of that by becoming more like him and less like the world.

*Oh Lord, your love is boundless, and your grace is sufficient for all my shortcomings. I will not abuse your kindness by indulging in sin, but instead accept it humbly and work towards change and growth.*

# GIFT OF GOD

*Thanks be to God for his indescribable gift!*
2 CORINTHIANS 9:15 NKJV

As undeserving as we are of God's incredible gifts, he gladly gives them. He is so generous and loving, he graciously pours out his blessings on his children. How can we begin to thank him for the gifts he has given to us, especially the gift of his Son? He is loving in every way. When times are hard, he picks us up. In seasons of plenty, he rejoices with us. His path is always clear, and his voice is calming. The raging sea becomes still in his presence, and the birds sing his praises.

In all his power, dominion, and wisdom, God chooses us to be the recipients of his gifts. His ultimate gift of sacrificing his own life so that we could live is truly indescribable. He is too great for words. By his grace, we are made whole, free, and forgiven.

*Jesus, perfect gift of God, you are my timeless treasure. I love you, and I thank you for the indescribable sacrifice you made for me. Thank you for choosing to lay down your life so that I can live with you forever.*

# NO MORE SORROW

*"He will wipe every tear from their eyes, and there will be no more death or sorrow or crying or pain. All these things are gone forever."*
REVELATION 21:4 NLT

Death will die. One day, it will happen. As crushing as our pain is, he will wipe away every tear from our eyes." This is not a possibility; it is certain. Christ does not tolerate pain and suffering, for nothing bad can abide with him. He is entirely good. That is why it is his ultimate plan to wipe away every mark of sadness and death so we can worship him in person for his complete victory.

This is our hope in times of suffering. This is what we hold on to when the pain, loss, and fatigue drag us down. Here on earth, Satan makes his presence known in all that detracts from life and joy. It our pleasure to remember that in heaven, God makes his presence known by the life and joy that will be fully present.

*Be my hope, Lord. Remind me that there will one day be no more sorrow, no more pain. When suffering gets to be too much, bring my mind back to this verse of hope.*

# SEE CLEARLY

*"You hypocrite! First, take the wood out of your own eye.*
*Then you will see clearly to take the dust out of your friend's eye."*
MATTHEW 7:5 NCV

Although our Lord graciously forgives us, we cannot expect to be granted such mercy if we refuse to extend the same forgiveness to others. Our Lord, as judge of heaven and earth, has decreed that love is to prevail. Our job is to obey him and leave him to do the judging. He is the only one qualified to judge the hearts of mankind. He created them, and he can execute perfect judgment and perfect mercy simultaneously.

If we are too busy judging others and noticing their flaws, we cannot see clearly enough to deal with our own problems or to help them with theirs. It should be an easy task to forgive other people of their offenses after we have been forgiven of so much.

*God, help me see clearly, so that I can mend my ways and then help others through their problems in a loving and gracious way. I want to treat other people the way you have treated me.*

# SOMETHING BETTER

*Let us stop going over the basic teachings about Christ again and again. Let us go on instead and become mature in our understanding. Surely we don't need to start again with the fundamental importance of repenting from evil deeds and placing our faith in God.*

HEBREWS 6:1 NLT

The first experience of repenting before God is a powerful one. It leaves a lasting impression of God's goodness toward us, how he turned away his own wrath, and how we were welcomed into his family. Unfortunately, our memory of this experience can be corrupted. We may equate it with closeness to God and aim for the same experience time and time again. We might think it is the only way we can come closer to God. But God has already forgiven us.

God has great things for us to learn about him. He wants to grow this relationship, but not through repeatedly laying a foundation of repentance from dead works. Instead, he wants us to learn how to separate good from evil (Hebrews 5:14), how to bring others to Christ, and how to leave behind all the traces of sin in our heart. Repentance is not the peak of our religious experience; it is the first rung of the ladder.

*Lord, be with me all the time. Whether in calmness or in tumult, be my guide and friend. Teach me to never seek after what I consider religion to be, but instead to solely seek you.*

# THE LORD'S PATIENCE

*The Lord is not slow about His promise, as some count slowness,*
*but is patient toward you, not willing for any to perish,*
*but for all to come to repentance.*

2 PETER 3:9 NASB

"Why so long?" we might ask. We deal with tragedy after tragedy, watching as the Lord is ignored again and again by the world. It is hard to stand the brokenness. This is a natural consequence of knowing Christ. By being near to the one who heals all things, we grow more aware of our world's brokenness. The question arises whether the Lord is slow about his promise to restore creation.

Christ desires all to be saved. If anything, the brokenness of our world is reason to hope Christ will not return too soon. There are still so many to save, so many destined for eternity without God. That is what Peter means when he says that God patient. He wants everyone to repent and live with him.

*God, give me a heart for the work yet to be done. Let the brokenness of society inspire me to show your love for all people. Today, may I also hope for all to come to repentance.*

# PEACE

*"Glory to God in the highest, and on earth peace
among those with whom he is pleased!"*
LUKE 2:14 ESV

This Christmas edict is common around churches and greeting
cards this time of year. Do we stop to consider the profound
implications of this proclamation? The angels declared peace to
the shepherds, not peace between us and our neighbors, or family
members, or even between countries. Since the beginning of
time, this world has been full of conflict and war, and that will not
change until the end of time.

The angels were declaring peace between us and the Almighty! We
are no longer at odds with our Creator because he bridged the gap.
He crossed the barrier of sin and came to us himself. He came to set
things right and bring us back home to him. He is pleased with us,
and he came himself to tell us so. Glory to God, the highest and the
holiest of all!

*Oh Father, thank you for reconciling me to you. Thank
you for stooping to my level, freeing me from sin, and
declaring peace between humanity and yourself. I will
glorify your name forevermore!*

# WISE PLANNING

*The plans of the diligent lead surely to plenty,*
*But those of everyone who is hasty, surely to poverty.*

PROVERBS 21:5 NKJV

There are so many great things we can do with our life. It is hard to dedicate ourselves when so many options are good. The writer of Proverbs warns us that the plans of "everyone who is hasty" leads "surely to poverty." With so many good paths to pursue, whether it is vocation or mission, there is still so much possibility for us to mess up.

What is there for us to do, then? "The plans of the diligent lead surely to plenty." The only thing we can do is dedicate our plans to the Lord, entrust them to him, and then attend to them as best as we can. There is no fool-proof way of assuring our success apart from living faithfully in diligence.

*How can I be diligent with my time today, God? Show me. Make me wise in planning, dedicated in pursuing your will, and faithful in trusting you with all my pursuits.*

# DIFFERENT TOGETHER

*Each one of us has a body with many parts, and these parts all have different uses. In the same way, we are many, but in Christ we are all one body. Each one is a part of that body, and each part belongs to all the other parts.*

ROMANS 12:4-5 NCV

It's easy to judge people who are different from us. Maybe their theological beliefs go against our own, or their lifestyle doesn't match our view of how things should be done. We must remember that God created us to be different. He didn't make a bunch of clones to live a certain way, eat the same foods every day, and listen to the same music. He created individuals to fulfill all kinds of purposes: missionaries, doctors, artists, grandparents, and every kind of role one could play.

To be different is to have the ability to impact someone's life in a positive and different way, and to add perspective to the world. We are all differently functioning units of one machine. For this machine to work, we must each pursue our God-given roles and support others in theirs.

*God, when I judge others for not acting or looking the same way as I do, remind me that we were not made to be the same. You have crafted a unique plan for each one of us, and our paths will look different. Help me to appreciate and celebrate the variety in your children.*

# TRIALS

*Do not be surprised at the fiery ordeal among you, which comes upon you for your testing, as though something strange were happening to you; but to the degree that you share the sufferings of Christ, keep on rejoicing, so that at the revelation of His glory you may also rejoice and be overjoyed.*

1 PETER 4:12-13 NASB

The devil would like to surprise us by the intensity of our pain, but Peter will not let us be fooled. Our trials are not strange, though they are fiery. This testing marks us as true Christians. Peter speaks as a fellow sufferer who knows the seriousness of tribulation. He encourages us with the reminder that we are not alone. The world does not hate us more than it did him.

We can thank God that he made the church a community. We are brothers and sisters in suffering, encouraging one another and upholding each other's tired souls. Just as Peter encouraged those he called beloved, we can encourage each other during times of pain.

*It will only be a little while, God. Remind me of this. May I not be stunned by tribulation, and may it instead move me to action in supporting others who are likewise afflicted. Thank you, God, for being my consolation in all circumstances.*

# PASSIONATE LOVE

*Christ proved God's passionate love for us*
*by dying in our place while we were still lost and ungodly!*
ROMANS 5:8 TPT

More than simply tell us how much he loves us, God shows us through every single act he has done. At the pinnacle of our sin, Christ died in our place, which is utterly impossible for our human minds to comprehend. Only a loving and flawless God could accomplish such a feat.

The passionate love of God is beyond any love that we have known. It was from God's love that all other loves were born, and from his death that we all have life. The knowledge that an all-powerful and holy God would reach down and cross the vast divide between us and him is astonishing. He proved his unyielding love when he paid for reconciliation with his own blood. Such is the unparalleled love of God.

*Great Redeemer, I am awed by your passionate and sacrificial love, which you bestow on us undeserving people. Help me to honor you by sharing your love with those around me.*

# GOOD JUDGMENT

*For every matter there is a time and judgment,*
*Though the misery of man increases greatly.*
ECCLESIASTES 8:6 NKJV

Our God loves order, and that's how he created things to work in the natural world. Everything happens in its time and season. There is no chaos or confusion in God's perfect creation. Sin disrupted the natural ebb and flow. James 3:16 says that, "Where envy and self-seeking exist, confusion and every evil thing are there." Disorder comes from the evil one and from our sinful decisions. We should recognize it as a warning sign, like a console light blinking in a car.

James goes on to conclude that, "The wisdom that is from above is first pure, then peaceable, gentle, willing to yield, full of mercy and good fruits, without partiality and without hypocrisy" (James 3:17). This is the world which God intended. Although the misery of mankind is great on the earth, we will one day return to perfect order.

*Lord, I look to you for clarity and peace in my life. You love order, and your ways are not confusing. Thank you for giving me your Word as a beacon in the darkness.*

# AWARENESS

*The wise see danger ahead and avoid it,*
*but fools keep going and get into trouble.*
PROVERBS 27:12 NCV

Staying aware of what's around you may sound like an obvious task, but it is often overlooked. We can get so caught up in our own lives that we fail to recognize what is going on in the lives of people around us. How often are we staring at our phones rather than engaging in face-to-face conversations? This sort of tunnel-vision is isolating and potentially dangerous. While navigating treacherous terrain, we need to have each other's backs and stay aware of patterns and people. Failing to do so could leave us alone and in trouble.

Sometimes our sinful, stubborn natures take precedence, and we choose the dangerous path instead of avoiding it. The Bible is full of practical, everyday advice, and we would be wise to be aware of it. Let us learn to the wisdom in this proverb and avoid danger. Foolish behavior causes unnecessary pain for us and often those close to us and being aware can remove that threat.

*Father, sometimes I am foolish and sinful and fall into*
*trouble. Teach me the truths of your Word so I can be aware*
*and wise.*

# SELFLESS SACRIFICE

*Going a little farther, he fell on the ground and prayed that,
if it were possible, the hour might pass from him. And he said, "
Abba, Father, all things are possible for you. Remove this cup from me.
Yet not what I will, but what you will."*

MARK 14:35-36 ESV

Even Jesus, in his ultimate perfection and infinite love, knew pain.
When the time was coming for him to be sacrificed, he prayed
and asked God to make another way. He didn't want to suffer, and
he didn't want to be separated from the Father. But after all the
turmoil, he still said that he wanted God's will to be done, and not
his own. When faced with the most painful spiritual experience
possible, Jesus still chose to honor God over his own will to live.

In our daily lives, we should strive to put God's will before ours and
choose to do things that will glorify him, not us. If we struggle, we
can remember that Jesus chose death to himself, so that we could
live with the Father. He gave us the freedom to deny ourselves, take
up our crosses, and follow him.

*Thank you, God, for Jesus' sacrifice. Your sacrifice. I know
that without it, I would not have the freedom I do now.
Teach me the importance of respecting your plan over my
own desires.*

# AFFLICTION AND COMFORT

*That we may be able to comfort those who are in any trouble,*
*with the comfort with which we ourselves are comforted by God.*
2 CORINTHIANS 1:4 NKJV

We have a comfort so profound that it overflows our souls and reaches the hearts of those around us. The God and Father of our Lord Jesus Christ is not so small that he would neglect our well-being. He is not limited in resources, so he doesn't give us just enough comfort to get by. Instead, he takes his grace and pours it out on us so that, even in our brokenness, we have joy that defies all human rationality.

God loves to accomplish his purposes in ways that we would not consider. Instead of offering comfort through put-together and well-off Christians, he offers it through those who are most broken.

*God, my affliction cannot be denied. Thank you for comforting me in it and helping me show that comfort to others. May I be encouraged today with the thought that my suffering allows me to comfort those around me who are afflicted in a similar way.*

# GOD IS ABLE

*"I know that You can do all things,*
*And that no plan is impossible for You."*
JOB 42:2 NASB

Most of us accept and believe that God is able to do all things. But do we wonder if he will? As we see evil progress and good people suffer, do we question where God is? In our heads, we know God is near, but our hearts lead us to feel all alone. Do we question how much he cares? When we pray, do we become disheartened when we don't hear an answer, or the answer we hoped for?

What if we opened our minds and our hearts to what God is actually doing? If we know that God is able and God is love, then he must have a plan. With his flawless track record and heavenly vantagepoint, we can conclude that his ways supersede our own. When we pray, let us go before our Maker, already convinced that he is fully capable and fully engaged in our lives, and ask for his help to play our part in his purposes.

*Almighty God, instead of becoming dismayed when you don't show up when I want and how I want, teach me what you want. Teach me your ways. My desire is to become a part of your perfect plan, so help me put my plans back in your capable hands.*

# SEASONS AND CHANGE

*A time to tear, and a time to sew;
a time to keep silence, and a time to speak.*
ECCLESIASTES 3:7 ESV

It is not always the right time for something. Grief and joy, speaking and silence, investing and gathering in, all have their time. Our greatest skill is knowing when one time has ended and another begins. Silence cannot always reign, especially when God calls us to speak up on his behalf. Similarly, talking must not dominate our interactions with others, or else we will have communication taking place of action. God, in his wisdom, has appointed a season for everything.

Do we embrace God's timing? Humans naturally want to be in control, but things do not always happen as we want them to. Sometimes it is a time to tear, and we want it to be a time to sew. But God has his own timing, and all we can do is trust his timing.

*Lord, help me to trust your plan. I am not in control, no matter how much I would like to be. I want to embrace your will and your appointed times. Teach me to place my assurance in you, rather than my control over my life. And please, forgive me when I, who am unworthy, attempt to take control from you, who are worthy.*

# SECURE LOVE

*In all these things we are more than conquerors through Him who loved us. For I am persuaded that neither death nor life, nor angels nor principalities nor powers, nor things present nor things to come, nor height nor depth, nor any other created thing, shall be able to separate us from the love of God which is in Christ Jesus our Lord.*

ROMANS 8:37-39 NKJV

Amid persecution, Paul reassured the church that nothing can separate us from the incredible love of God. Over the last two thousand years, God's love has not changed. We have the same assurance that no matter how terrible things become and regardless of our circumstances, God will never forsake us.

We are more than conquerors because Christ has already won the war! It is a long, slow road to victory, but the outcome is certain and in our favor. Nothing in this intervening time can come between us and the everlasting, unwavering, unchanging love of God.

*Even when we were your enemies, you loved me. Now that I am your child, will you not continue to hold onto me and love me dauntlessly? Your love is certain and secure; in that I place all my hope.*

# BIRTH OF OUR SAVIOR

*A child has been born to us; God has given a son to us.*
*He will be responsible for leading the people.*
*His name will be Wonderful Counselor, Powerful God,*
*Father Who Lives Forever, Prince of Peace.*

ISAIAH 9:6 NCV

Approximately 700-800 years before Jesus was born, Isaiah wrote that it would happen. This wasn't a guess or wishful thinking; God consistently imparted future events to Isaiah so he could help the people of Israel. There are many times in the Bible when God tells his people that a redeemer will come from among them. They had all sorts of ideas about who this redeemer would be, and how he would go about saving them.

When Jesus finally did come, many didn't believe in him. They thought he would come in power and destroy their Roman oppressors. Jesus, however, came quietly as a little baby in a stable, surrounded only by his parents, some shepherds, and a few animals. He taught the people about peace and servitude, patience and selflessness. He didn't match their idea of a savior. Jesus will not fit into the box we've created in our heads, but he will wildly surpass our greatest hopes and desires.

*God, thank you for the example of humility and grace that Jesus set for me. I often think I know better, but time and again you show me that power rests in your hands, and that is the safest place for it. Thank you for giving me exactly what I need.*

# BORN TO YOU

*"Today in the town of David a Savior has been born to you;*
*he is the Messiah, the Lord."*
LUKE 2:11 NIV

The day Christ was born in Bethlehem was the day when perfect strength and perfect humility were joined forever. Jesus could not have been our Savior if he did not understand what it was like to be like us. So, he was born in Bethlehem to become exactly like us in humanness. He was unlike us, however, in how perfectly he lived the life of a person. We are tainted by pride and corrupted desires, but Christ was perfectly humble and compassionate.

To be our perfect Savior, he also needed to have God's power to save, which meant he had to be fully God. If he had not been perfectly holy, he could not have lived as a perfect human being. This would have made him an insufficient offering. There is no union as perfect as the joining of human and heavenly natures that occurred in Bethlehem that first Christmas day.

*Lord Jesus, I thank you this day for what you have done. Thank you for arriving in weakness to prove yourself mighty, to wash away my sins and make a way to the Father. Unto me you were born, Lord. Unto you I offer my thankful praise.*

# STAND VICTORIOUS

*I have saved these most important truths for last:*
*Be supernaturally infused with strength through your life-union*
*with the Lord Jesus. Stand victorious with the force of his explosive*
*power flowing in and through you.*
EPHESIANS 6:10 TPT

Every day, we engage in spiritual battles, and Paul did not shy away from that point when he was writing to the church in Ephesus. They are so real and important that Paul saved some important tactics for overcoming them for the end of his letter.

Our strength is supernatural because it comes from the Lord. In ourselves, we do not have the power or strength to overcome sin and darkness. With the light of Christ in us, the victory is ours, and nothing can bring us down. God is standing near, ready to give us everything we need to overcome. We only need to pray in faith and ask.

*Without you, Lord Jesus, I do not stand a chance against the impending darkness. I am not strong enough to even overcome my own sins and weaknesses. But by your grace and with your strength, I gratefully claim victory and stand in freedom, ready to follow you wherever you lead.*

# INTENTIONALITY

*Be careful how you walk, not as unwise people but as wise,*
*making the most of your time, because the days are evil.*
Ephesians 5:15-16 nasb

If anyone was well-acquainted with the possibility of death, it was the apostle Paul. He had been shipwrecked, stoned, beaten, imprisoned, and homeless, and he recognized that his days were numbered by the Lord. He lived intentionally because he did not know which day would be his last.

Although we may not have lives as tumultuous as Paul's, the truth is that we also do not know when our last day on this earth will be. Life is full of distractions and schemes of the enemy looking to lull us into an apathetic state of temporal living. Paul cautioned us to be careful how we walk. We are to make the most of our time and live intentionally. Evil prevails in this world, so we walk in wisdom and do not get caught up in it as unwise people do. Our time here is short, so how can we use it for God?

*Gracious Lord, thank you for the gift of life! May my life reflect your love and may the wisdom you give set me apart from the foolishness of the world.*

# NOT FORGOTTEN

*"Can a woman forget the baby she nurses?*
*Can she feel no kindness for the child to which she gave birth?*
*Even if she could forget her children, I will not forget you."*

ISAIAH 49:15 NCV

We have all seen the way a mother reacts to her crying baby. It is hard for her to focus on anything else when her baby starts to call. Even if she is engrossed in another activity, the very sound of her infant causes a mental, emotional, and physical reaction from her. There is no ignoring a crying baby. She doesn't forget to nurse her baby, because her body is tied to the needs of her child. The love she feels for her baby, who has done nothing to deserve her love other than exist, engulfs her entire existence. She would do anything to protect and care for her child.

This self-sacrificing, unexplainable love did not originate with us. Like every other good thing, its author is God. The love a mother feels for her child may seem incredible, but it is only a reflection of the love God feels for his children. It would be easier to imagine a mother with no kindness for the child she birthed than it would be to imagine that God could forget about and abandon us.

*You are my devoted and loving Father. I rejoice in knowing that I am not forgotten—not ever.*

# HUMBLE HONOR

*Humble yourselves under the mighty power of God,*
*and at the right time he will lift you up in honor.*
1 PETER 5:6 NLT

God did not create us to be copies of each other. He did not want identical, carbon copy servants. He wanted unique, significant children, and he wanted personal relationships with each one. He made each of us special and in his image. Imagine how vast and incredible God must be if each of us is a fragmented reflection of his glory and splendor.

God made us for honor, not disgrace. We naturally desire honor. But if we try to achieve honor in a less than honorable way, it opposes God's better intentions. When we humble ourselves and give all glory to God, he will in his time and way lift us up in honor. We must trust God's timing instead of trying to demand or force it. Honor is given, not taken.

*How humbling it is simply to know that I have been created in your image! To bear the image of my Father, King, and Creator is an unfathomable honor.*

# MERCY

*"His mercy extends to those who fear him,
from generation to generation."*
LUKE 1:50 NIV

Fearing God does not mean fearing his punishment. This is an unrighteous fear that leads to legalism rather than a life of grace. Considering this, fearing God more closely means revering God. When we stand before the throne of God, we may quiver at his presence, but it will be out of a sense of awe rather than fear.

If you stand in awe of your Savior, if you acknowledge him in times of doubt, in times of fear; if you refuse to ignore him when those around you do, and if you revere him in your conduct, it will not go unnoticed. God is not so cruel as to mistreat the children he has raised up in faithfulness. He will protect you, provide for you, and shed his mercy on you time and time again. In the words of Mary's prayer, he will do this "from generation to generation."

*Lord, encourage me to fear you righteously. Help me to not fear your punishment or disapproval. Today, may I stand in awe of all that you are, robed in strength, glory, and mercy.*

# STEADFAST LOVE

*The Lord will fulfill his purpose for me;*
*your steadfast love, O Lord, endures forever.*
*Do not forsake the work of your hands.*
PSALM 138:8 ESV

When the Lord says he will do something, he will do it. He does not forget or forsake the work he has started in us. We may rest assured that he will fulfill his purposes in us. What he has started, he will finish. Our Father does not give us a task and then abandon us to figure it out on our own; he walks with us and sees it through to completion. His love is perfectly steadfast, and we can rest upon it.

Whatever purposes the Lord planted in your heart, he will accomplish them. As long as we stay willing, humble, and obedient to God, we can have confidence in our purposes coming to fruition. We don't need to force things or hurry the process along. God knows perfectly what he is doing.

*Your steadfast love, dear Lord, speaks of your character.*
*Not only are you loving, but everything you do is consistently*
*and dependably loving. I trust you fully to work in me, and I*
*open my heart to you.*